PRAISE FOR
A SOUL'S SU

MW01001371

Out of the Box, A Soul's Surprising Journey is an intimate, conversational, practical guide for the spiritual traveler. The poignant stories from Barbara's soul healing experiences offer valuable teachings about how our Divine self, our guides, and our teachers continually help us to master the curriculum of our life. What an uplifting book!

~Marci Shimoff, NY Times bestselling author, *Happy for No Reason* and *Chicken Soup for the Woman's Soul*

From the heart of time comes a story of remembrance, recognition, and renewal. *Out of the Box, A Soul's Surprising Journey* is a timeless ordering of divinely directed events, messages, and understandings that bring the full promise of grace to a world that is questing for truth, justice, and acceptance. Balancing the light and the dark as a finely woven fabric, Lucerne reflects on the relationship between our free will choice, the intention of our hearts, and the need for pure awareness and innate balance as we stand amidst the tides of change and upheaval. As we support and uphold all as divine, we again are one with the earth, the mother, and the Absolute—reflections of the light within that guide us home.

~Flo Aeveia Magdalena, author of *I Remember Union: The Story of Mary Magdalena; Sunlight on Water: A Guide for Soul-full Living;* and *Honoring Your Child's Spirit: Pre-birth Bonding and Communication.*

This book will touch your heart and soul as you relate to the stories and the personal lessons experienced by Barbara. You will know with certainty that you are not alone in what you have been experiencing! This masterful storyteller provides a framework for understanding how the multifaceted layers of past, present, and future converge to produce the manifestations of loveless thoughts, feelings and actions with which each of us struggles. More than that, she tells us how to individually and collectively deal with and overcome them so that we can herald in the new age of 1,000 years of peace, love and prosperity. Barbara's true essence shines through this book. She gives a piece of herself with each telling of her experiences and the understandings gained through them.

Serving as your guide, she shares with you simple ways to become empowered. Masterful and entertaining, this book contains what you need to be able to say, "I get it and I now know what I need to do!"
~Gabrielle Spencer
Spiritual Intuitive Guide
Initiations & Activations for Spiritual Evolution

"Thank you for writing so generously and candidly of your life experiences that led to you being the sparkly goddess that you are now. These tender sharings, so sweetly woven, inspire the reader to look more closely at all the threads that so richly form our own personal tapestry of life."
~Diana Rose, Guide to the Casa de Dom Inacio

As the chapters pass, each piece of Barbara's life puzzle fits together to bring awareness and hope that the power of prayer will allow good to triumph over the forces of evil during this time of uncertainty on Earth. Barbara's spiritual journey educates and shines a bright light on how to proceed as loving souls to complete God's plan for us.
~Lynne Jackson DaRos, M.A., Holistic Counseling

Out of the Box:

A Soul's Surprising Journey

Barbara Lucerne Woolley

Everyone who has ever been a part of my life has contributed to this story. I am eternally grateful to each one of you. While looping in and out of one another's lives, we have all been the beneficiaries of lessons that can only come through human existence. Sometimes we have loved each other. Sometimes we have not liked one another much at all. No matter what, no one can deny that we have been having a grand adventure! For this, fellow travelers, I say thank you with all my heart. I dedicate this book to each of you. I dedicate this book to everyone who chooses to stand strong and true on the path of love.

I especially dedicate this book to my wonderful children for traveling the ride of the Mad Hatter whether you wanted to or not. I love you more than you can imagine. Thank you for loving me no matter what.

Out of the Box, A Soul's Surprising Journey could not have been published without the selfless assistance of Joan Engel, Hollis Melton, Nancy Strachan, Jean Goudie, and Lynne Jackson DaRos. Your wise insights, encouragement, honest editing and get it done cheerleading have encouraged me to cross the finish line. Thank you. You have each definitely earned a hefty batch of brownie points in heaven!

With deep gratitude,

Lucerne

Table of Contents

INTRODUCTION

Out of the Box, A Soul's Surprising Journey tells stories of the recovery of parts of my soul that were waiting for me to find them in distant places and times. After a period of intense immersion in therapeutic work pertaining to this lifetime, the focus of my efforts suddenly exploded to include the healing of my soul. Ever since, the field of play has included arenas I could never have imagined. A big wake-up event was required to set what you will read about in motion.

The stories in the book have unfolded over many years and over many lifetimes. All come from direct experience. While I have changed some details to ensure the privacy of certain individuals, what is written is the truth as I have experienced it. I have had to learn patience for the pieces of the puzzle book in which I live to fall into place. This has been a nail-biting, on the edge of the seat, by the seat of the pants, on a wing and a lot of prayers adventure! More than a few years ago I realized that I am not the one steering the canoe even though I appear to be sitting in the stern, paddle in hand. I have come to trust (most of the time) that a plan is at work within and around me that knows better than I do when, where, what, and how something is to be revealed.

The types of encounters and retrievals described are not unique to me, thank goodness. Before 1985, I would have thought such stories to be wonderful works of fiction. Some are definitely hard to believe. The words below, inscribed upon a statue of St. Ignatius at the Casa de Dom Inacio, Abadiania, Brazil, comfort my heart when I encounter skepticism and judgmental disbelief:

For those who believe, no words are necessary.
For those who do not believe, no words are possible.
~St. Ignatius

We humans are surely a complex composite of experiences. Each of us carries the residue of unfinished karma, teachings of the ages, and abilities and gifts from other lifetimes, all deftly interwoven with our spiritual lineage, our soul remembrances, and our physical ancestry. These three streams of connection flow constantly like an underground river to direct and influence us from moment to moment. Our lives are the point of convergence for these mighty rivers. Affecting us also is whatever is moving in the world at large and in the collective conscious and unconscious. The mix is therefore complicated as well as in a continual state of change. Part of our assignment is to resolve, heal, and clear the residues that come into our fields from these arenas. On the one hand, we might say, well, if that is not mine, why do I need to deal with it? Yet, if you accept the notion that we all come from the One—a cellular mitosis type of a situation—and we are returning to the One, then it behooves us to accept such assignments. In this sense, each of us bears responsibility for the whole. This is what makes life a treasure to be cherished and so very interesting.

The stories begin with an incident that stirred the awakening of my soul. For the next few years, I remained a reluctant riser from a nap that began in antiquity. Eventually, enough momentum gathered to bring on lessons and blessings I needed to provoke me out of that sleepy state. *Out of the Box, A Soul's Surprising Journey* has been written to encourage those of you who are similarly reluctant, perhaps even fearful, to make your wake-up call. What I am certain of is that, for each of us, *the* work of the time is the reclamation and expansion of our soul. The purpose of this book is to reassure you, by sharing anecdotes from my journey, that there truly is a light at the end of the tunnel, and, to emphasize how supported we are every step of the way—even when we make mistakes. There is no doubt that I have made some gigantic mistakes. Those "errors" have yielded profound, unforgettable lessons. One of my primary teachers, White Waters, told me that he loves to make mistakes because he learns from them. His wisdom works for me!

Please understand from the outset that these are *my* stories. You may never have some of the encounters I have had. Other stories, however, may be relevant to the learning modules that are included in your spiritual curriculum. With soul awakening come lessons that are sometimes out of this world. Tips for negotiating those uncharted waters are part of this offering. You have your own story, your own travel plans, and your own individualized educational plans scripted over eons of time. I trust that you will find your personal odyssey a fascinating one.

Perhaps a true story from one escapade might inspire you to be a more active participant in the story that is your life. The year was 1993. I had traveled with a group of people to Quebec, Canada, to canoe the remote, wild waters of the Dumoine River. We were dropped with our canoes onto the water from floatplanes. The beginning was exciting, and an apt metaphor for how we as spirit drop onto this physical planet all pumped up for the grand adventure of a lifetime! The first day was spent learning and practicing white water canoe techniques before we plunged into absolute wilderness replete with rapids of varying class size.

I was proud owner and wearer of a brand new pair of great looking hiking shoes—they were tan with electric blue and hot pink stripes down the sides. I loved those boots. I tried hard not to ruin them by getting them wet. That fear had a history. When I was a young child, I ruined my brand new black patent leather Sunday school shoes by making footprints in a neighbor's freshly poured cement sidewalk. As a young teen, while running around in the woods one night during a pajama party, I lost half of a new pair of shoes. My parents were not mean, but I remembered their disapproval.

Stressed out by the middle of the second day of paddling, I realized I was not having much fun because I was spending far too much time worrying about ruining the yet unblemished boots. The effect was that I literally walked only the edges of the adventure. I had not yet become a full, enthusiastic participant. Had I traveled such a great distance only to shy away from this once-in-a-lifetime opportunity? Realistically, there was no way the boots were not going to get wet. There was no way that the entirety of me was not going to get wet. I had signed up for an innately wet type of a trip. No longer willing to remain a bystander, I impulsively jumped into the river, got those sucker shoes and myself all good and wet. This decisive immersion opened me to one of the most amazing wilderness trips of my life. Eight glorious days in nature with incredible challenges, incredible accomplishments, incredible beauty, over a hundred black fly sneak-attack bites, and two nutty tent mates who would not go to bed until they had euthanized each and every mozzie (Australian for mosquito).

Please do not be afraid to get your boots wet! Jump into the great river of your life. Sure, you'll get soaked. Sure, there are rapids that will toss you every which way to knock you off course. Sometimes you may be paddling a canoe full of water as you watch your gear float down river. So what! Just learn to giggle when those moments happen. Be thankful for the lessons. You will learn a lot about yourself, about what truly matters, and what just does not. The river absolutely knows where to take you.

~Silent Woman

PART ONE
OFF WITH THE LID!

REBIRTH

I arrived one month early in 1947. Placenta previa, a situation in which the placenta prematurely disconnects from the walls of the uterus, was the culprit. Medical research has well documented the link between cigarette smoking and placenta previa. My mother smoked two packs of cigarettes a day. Weighing in at four pounds four ounces with see-through fingers and toes, I remained a captive in an incubator for five weeks. Western childbirth practices in 1947 were very different than they are now. There were no warnings to expectant mothers about the dangers to the fetus of cigarette smoking. Mothers were drugged unconscious, therefore made non-participant in the bringing of their children into the world. The concept of mother-infant bonding was not yet recognized. My mother, initially sent home on bed rest for two weeks, came to visit when she could. The resultant emotional distance between us lasted thirty-eight years.

During meditation near the end of the second day of an "Inner Child" workshop led by Dr. Charles Whitfield in New York City in 1985, I spontaneously began to relive my birth. The process went on for hours and continued well after the workshop ended. Fortunately, a colleague stayed with me until the experience, which was deep, conscious, and breathtakingly physical, concluded. Throughout this surprising event, I observed my birth in a state of co-consciousness both as incoming spirit and as adult witness. I felt and saw it all, including the emotional disconnect of my mother from me before, during, and after my birth. I understood without doubt that I, as spirit, could choose to come into the body to be born, or not. I saw that this birth and life would be difficult. I witnessed the decision-making process, how my spirit considered the pros and cons before recommitting to being born. I actually felt myself move down and out the birth canal. Entry into the stark hospital environment caused me to gasp for air. Mom and Dad named me Barbara, which means "warrior." This apt moniker correctly declared my resolve to fight for my life. Names truly can define the trajectory of our lives, as you will see. What I remembered next was the consoling presence of my loving father. He came to see me every day. I realized during the birth review why I had bonded with him rather than with my mother. I had often wondered about our closeness, why it stood in such sharp contrast to the perpetually distanced relationship between my mother and me.

Dad was a deeply devout Methodist and intimately involved in the inner workings of our local church. As a health care professional, he helped the underprivileged, especially children with birth defects. A humble man, he was highly regarded in the community for his kindness and gentleness. While Dad certainly had some glaring warts and pimples like the rest of us, his redeeming qualities were outstanding. His loving way surely helped me as newborn adjust to life in the physical after such a precipitous entry.

During the eulogy at his funeral, the pastor likened Dad to St. Barnabas. Since my friends and I had spent a considerable amount of time while attending church school making paper airplanes, writing gossipy notes, and seeking ways to escape the then boring teachings, the reference to St. Barnabas meant nothing to me. A recent trip to Turkey followed by the writing of this book renewed curiosity about the remark. Who was St. Barnabas? I hastened to the computer to perform an internet search. Barnabas, it turns out, was one of the earliest Christian disciples in Jerusalem. He traveled with Paul throughout Anatolia (Turkey) and other regions to preach the message of Master Jesus. Together they converted and successfully defended Gentile Christians against stricter church leaders who would reinstate Judaic practices, including circumcision. Circumcision was not part of Gentile religious or health practices. Barnabas died a martyr at Salamis, Cyprus in 61 A.D.[1] Known for his loving disposition, St. Luke described Barnabas as "a good man, a man full of the Holy Ghost and of Faith."[2] The online commentary helped me appreciate the high regard the pastor had for my father.

Mom stood on the doorstep waiting for me when I returned home from the workshop. I knew we needed to talk about what happened. I was not looking forward to this because my mother was emotionally avoidant to the extreme. Witnesses could testify to my playfully chasing her around the dinner table to get her to state her opinion about something. While we giggled during such moments, her reluctance to speak her truth was frustrating. This night she totally surprised me. She listened with full attention. She did not pooh-pooh one piece of the story as psychobabble. She verified absolutely everything I told her, then, looked me square in the eyes and said, "Yes, I know, and I'm so sorry." This was the biggest healing moment of my life. With her admission and apology, we were able to enjoy the final two years of her life. My mother died from metastatic lung cancer in 1987. Since crossing back over into spirit she has proven to be a wonderfully loving mother who makes her presence known from the other side primarily when I am in trouble in my heart or headed into danger.

Reliving my birth turned out to be the "thawing out" I had somehow always known would happen. Even as a young girl, I would tell people that I was "frozen in time" and that one day I would become "unfrozen." I did not know what that meant, but I sure knew it to be fact. The frozen state included a seemingly unchangeable youthful appearance. People used to express disbelief when told my true age. Alas, this state of captured youth gave way when the ice that enshrouded me melted! It took quite a while to realize that the thawing process initiated by the birth replay actually began the reawakening of my soul. With the dissolution of my personal Ice Age came an enormous shift in perception. An unstoppable process was set in motion. Trying to turn back, slow, or ignore the unfolding has proven impossible and certainly not desirable.

One year later—1986—I attended another symposium for therapists in Washington, D.C. I chose to participate in a guided meditation that was one of the course offerings. The facilitator took us down into a deep state of relaxation. Instantly and without conscious intent, I jetted into the place where the rebirth experience ended the year before. It was as though there had been no lapse in time whatsoever. What I did not tell you before is that, at the end of the 1985 rebirth event, I walked off into the desert, staff in hand, my baby self in a backpack on my back.

On this day, the visionary experience picked up precisely where it had left off. I journeyed through the dusty desert wilderness for forty years, then emerged onto a mountainous property named Capon Springs and Farms, a nature-based retreat center located in West Virginia that my family thoroughly enjoyed visiting when I was a child. My own children appeared in the Capon Springs vision with me, but not my husband. Repeatedly I tried to pull him into the picture with us, but all attempts to do so were unsuccessful. He remained irretrievably on the other side of the river. With a flash of insight, I knew without hesitation that our paths had diverged, that our marriage was over. Three years later, in 1989, I woke up one morning knowing in my bones that the time for separation had arrived. Ever since, I have wholeheartedly pursued my spiritual path.

Set free through the healing rebirth experience followed by my mother's honest acknowledgment of the true circumstances of my birth, I "grew up" while wandering in the desert for one year. Ready for the next step in the process, the second visionary experience brought me fully into present time. The Moses journey had prepared me to leave a marriage that no longer served either my husband or me in spite of our deep love for and commitment to our children. Much later, I came to understand that my mother's masterful emotional absence from me was intentional from a soul perspective. My father and I needed to heal an ancient trauma that took many years to unravel. His loving presence from the moment of my birth and throughout my life was part of his karmic debt to me. I know that he truly loved me. However, there were peculiarities and discomforts in our relationship during this lifetime that stemmed from events that actually took place thousands of years ago. I had to go through a whole lot more shaking and awakening to get the facts of that story.

VISION QUEST

1990 was yet another year for big revelations. I traveled to Northern Ontario to participate in grown-up camp on a remote island located in Lake Temagami. The island is accessed either by boat or by four-passenger floatplane. I took the plane. I was in awe as we flew above broccoli trees to circle-land onto the pristine, potable, windswept waters. The entrance was grand. This was my first out-of-country experience. Little did I know what had been set in motion when I responded to the invitation on the three by five card posted on a clinical school bulletin board. No details provided, the note card simply announced a seven-day Jungian-oriented Vision Quest experience and who to contact.

Having sat on myself almost my whole life, now ready for new experiences, I jumped at the opportunity. I had vowed at the end of my twenty-year marriage not to leave one stone unturned. Life was to be lived, not just read about in tales of adventure written by others. I was now the adventurer! What you don't know won't hurt you, right? Truthfully, I was clueless about the deep changes that were percolating within as I traveled to Lake Temagami. This, it turns out, was good. There were no preconceived notions to discard. I did not know that this journey would become the next great leap, one that turned me up, down, inside out and shot me out of the cannon at warp speed. My big concern beforehand was a fear of attack by bears while out on Vision Quest. However, the bear fear dissipated while riding bikes one evening with a friend with the realization that human beings are truly far more dangerous than most bears.

The quiet wilderness environment thoroughly enriched the dream-work process. I enjoyed learning about Native American teachings as our group prepared for Inipi (purification lodge) and for Vision Quest. When we slipped into the cold lake waters in the dark of night to cool our highly heated bodies after the purification lodge, I simply, joyfully, and without pre-thought traveled out of body to merge in ecstatic oneness with the sparkling Milky Way. I was home. I remembered oneness with God in that exquisite moment of bliss. I heard and felt the song of the universe. When called back by the leader, I reluctantly returned to my physical body. The sensation as my essence re-entered the body from head to toe was a strange one.

Inipi set the stage for the Vision Quest. When it was time, we paddled across the lake in pairs, tucked our canoes securely along shore, and parted paths to walk off alone in search of just the right spot in which to sit for two days. This was a modified Vision Quest—two days alone without water and food. I had something to cover my body, tissues, rain gear, a sleeping bag, a journal, and a flashlight—just in case. Following instructions, I cleared and set my spot, then began to sing and pray for a vision. Stripped down to near nakedness, the experience was a rare date in nature without interference.

Quickly I lost track of time. Hunger and thirst gave way to increasing appreciation of the world around me. The spirit within me soared. Hummingbird hovered above during a brief visit. The Mayans consider this little avian pollinator of joy to be a harbinger of the Fifth World. The next world to come for humanity, it will be a world of harmony and unity.[3] Water slurped as it lapped the edges of the shoreline. Trees made squeaking noises as their trunks and branches rubbed against each other in the wind. Some determined chattering red squirrels taught me how to harvest pinecones for the cold winter ahead. They worked all day and from every conceivable angle with an obvious resolve to leave not one pinecone behind! A slender black snake with lime green racing stripes slithered to the outer edge of my medicine circle, said hello with a bob of the head, then slid off down the path. I was awestruck by the abundant life that surrounded me. A clear, crisp, short and to the point communication had begun, one that was beyond the spoken word.

Late the second night, while sitting on a cliff that overlooked the lake, watching as stars began to pop in the midnight blue sky, the song, "Amazing Grace," just rose right up out of me. The powerful words of this profound song of gratitude for the reclamation of the soul that had been lost and now found reverberated deeply through every part of me. My lost soul—that I had not known had been lost—was found. I knew it. Thank God. A tangible, comforting presence gently moved in to sit behind me, just behind my left shoulder. She was an indigenous grandmother. Her soft voice joined with mine, we sang together until the song was complete.

English Anglican clergyman, John Newton, wrote and published "Amazing Grace" in 1779. The message of this song is one of forgiveness and redemption, that the soul can be delivered from despair through the mercy of God no matter what sins have been committed. Newton's wake-up call came during a terrible storm during a slave-trading voyage. Though non-religious, he was terrified and called upon God for help. A few years later, he left slave trading and the sea to begin the study of theology.[4]

What more could possibly happen? Full from Vision Quest, overflowing with gratitude and a renewed sense of self, I returned home assuming that the quest was complete. One weekend afternoon in the month that followed, while meditatively dancing in my spacious bedroom, the realms opened up again. With eyes wide open, I watched a small, gray-haired Native American woman ride into my bedroom on a brown and white Pinto horse. Her gray braids hung down her front alongside her sweet round, wrinkled, brown-skinned face. Was she real? She allowed me to touch her braids in response to my unspoken question. I needed to know that she was real. She looked at me with kind twinkling eyes, then she and her horse turned around to leave. As they departed, the horse left a deposit on the floor: a mound of inter-dimensional shit. Shocked, I wondered what it meant when one is gifted a pile of manure. When the vision ended, the grandmother, the horse, and the shit disappeared from my bedroom. One of the greatest, strangest gifts I have ever received, this vision guided and taught me well for nineteen years.

Native American ceremony opened doors previously elusively closed. It took me to my spiritual home, restored my soul and my faith in that indefinable something that foundations, permeates, supports, loves, and guides absolutely everything and everyone. Native American ceremony brought me to in-the-bones remembrance of God from the inside out. Now I was ready for my teachers to appear.

WHITE WATERS

Not long after I came back from Vision Quest, a friend asked if I wanted to attend a weekend class in shamanic healing. I signed up with great anticipation. After Canada, I was ready to learn all I could about indigenous healing ways. The teacher was Alberto Aguas, well-known healer from Sao Paolo, Brazil, who was an ardent advocate for the indigenous people and rainforests of the Amazon, Like pretty much everyone else, I fell in love with him on the spot. Handsome, utterly charming, and obviously cultured, he spoke with the sensuous Brazilian Portuguese accent I have so come to appreciate through my frequent travels to Brazil. While humorous, Alberto was also definitely serious as he took us through initiation into a spirit-guided system of healing named Ama Deus, which means "to love God."

Alberto's presence was enormous and intoxicating. His heart touched my heart deeply. I felt somehow profoundly connected to him. It was not until later that I realized I had been having my own unique experience with him in the midst of the group experience. Probably others were also having their own distinct encounters with him. All I know is that I saw him dressed in an Oriental blue jacket, although, as later reported by friends, he had apparently worn a woolen sports jacket, slacks, and a white shirt. Like a slide show, his appearance and dress changed to reflect different historical periods. Evidently, we'd known each other in different lifetimes. One such time was the French Revolution. Through the "slide show," he established our connection.

During a subsequent healing session with Alberto, I sank immediately into a deep trance state. At the end of the session, he was obviously frustrated that I did not get something he wanted me to understand or remember. Energy drunk when I slid off the table, I staggered out to a sofa in the waiting room and passed out stone cold for about forty-five minutes. I had never before experienced anything like this. I knew nothing about spiritual masters, those highly evolved souls who come to teach and serve among us. The high voltage energy that runs through them is incredible. Alberto was one such beautiful soul.

Alberto passed on in July, 1992. The night he died, I woke up with a start, knowing that someone had absolutely kicked me in the butt. The experience was so physical that I wrote it down in my bedside journal even though I did not understand who did it or why. When later told that he had crossed over, I also learned that he kicked a lot of butt on his way out. Each of us so fortunate apparently got that dramatic, unforgettable impetus to get going.

Alberto is in the spirit world now. There his name is White Waters. If you ask for Alberto Aguas, you'll get a "Who?" response. Interestingly enough, Aguas means waters. He cryptically kept part of his spiritual identity by choosing incarnation in a family with this last name. As the master teacher for Ama Deus Healing and more, White Waters continues to serve humanity from the world of spirit.

I am a grateful recipient of the lessons and encouragement he continues to offer from the other side. When I began to travel the world in 1997, he would manifest into the physical to punctuate an event or give a teaching as I traveled to places like Egypt, Tibet, New Zealand, Brazil, Peru, and even LL Bean in Freeport, Maine, and a ladies' room at JFK International Airport. Advanced souls can do these things. As a bodhisattva, he is a soul who has learned and graduated from his earthly lessons. Such souls remain in our sector to help us progress. Because they are advanced, they are able to do things we cannot. Like the time he showed up in a women's room at JFK to show me how to wash my hands and arms as preparation for prayer Islam-style. Or the day in Lima, Peru, when he appeared as a tour guide and specifically asked our group leader if he could sit next to me during lunch. On that occasion, I knew who sat beside me. Often though, I would "get it" only a millisecond after he disappeared back into the ethers, like the time in Egypt when our group was preparing to climb Mt. Sinai. That evening he showed up as a Bedouin, dressed appropriately in long flowing garb. He came over, shook my hand firmly, wished me well on the middle-of-the-night pilgrimage, and smiled warmly. Dumbstruck, I just shook his hand back. When I came to my senses, he was gone.

White Waters' appearance in a town near where I lived was the start of an enduring, rich, learning relationship with a master teacher. He has systematically and steadfastly guided me ever since. In all honesty, I do not know what I would have done over the years without his constant, reassuring, humorous, sensitive, sometimes stern, provocative presence.

Next came Grandmother Twylah Nitsch, Seneca Elder and head of the Wolf Clan Teaching Lodge of the Seneca Indian Historical Society. Gram lived on the Cattaraugus Indian Reservation just south of Buffalo, New York. A year before I met her I had a lucid dream of a purposeful, small-statured, gray-hair-in-a-bun Native American grandmother who insisted that I lay down on a wheel of twelve different colors. I drew the wheel in my journal, described her appearance, and left it at that. I did not know who she was. It took the entire year that followed to find out.

During clinical supervision one summer day in 1991, the supervisor and I somehow diverged onto the topic of Native American teachings. She told me about a book written by a physical therapist she knew that contained color wheel teachings learned from the author's indigenous teacher. During my drive home, a huge rainbow appeared in the sky. Without difficulty, I was able to get hold of a copy of the book. To my amazement, I found the teacher's contact information in the back of the book. I called right away. Within a couple of weeks, a friend and I traveled to the Cattaraugus Reservation to attend our first weekend intensive with Grandmother Twylah.

What a weekend! As we entered her property, we heard a wolf howl. My friend and I looked at each other, knowing that we had driven into something beyond our usual reality. Gram was warm and approachable. Intent upon her mission, she got right down to the business of teaching about the Cycles of Truth and the Pathway of Peace. She did not agree with the style of Vision Quest in which I had participated. Her belief was that the experience could be much gentler. I had not thought that the experience lacked gentleness. I loved every moment and was deeply grateful for what had happened for me. Confused, I backed off a bit. I also was rather shook up by maps of the world that greeted us boldly the moment we stepped into her home. The maps showed what the United States might look like after the Earth Changes, the prophesied time of earthquakes, weather changes and pole shift. My home state was under water. Salt Lake City sat on the Bay of Tranquility.

Overwhelmed, at lunchtime I announced to my friend that I was out of there. I would find a motel, come back to pick her up Sunday afternoon. This was rather uncharacteristic for me. A long-hauler, I would not ordinarily give thought to leaving any relationship or event for which I had I signed up. Gram was definitely the grandmother of my dreams—she looked the same and taught what I saw in the dream. She was also quite precisely plucking every one of my nerves. Still working on mother issues—truthfully, looking for a surrogate mother—I had hoped she would be more motherly. Gram was not about to let me attach to her in that way, I could tell. Anyway, I took a nap in lieu of leaving. That helped. After lunch, we received our Creature Teachers—our animal helpers. One of mine happened to be Goat. No explanation needed. Well, I just started to laugh and laugh and then laugh more. Gram and everyone else did, too. With that uncontrollable cathartic release, I was over "it" and the rest of the weekend was just wonderful.

The trip home was adventuresome. As soon as we drove out of Gram's driveway, we found ourselves on a road we did not recognize. This set the tone for the entire rest of the inexplicably long trip. We just could not seem to get onto the interstate. We could drive parallel to it, but all attempts to reach the Pennsylvania Turnpike failed. We had no choice but to stay with the parallel course—the road less traveled. Around midnight, we drove into the parking lot of a bowling alley in Reading, Pennsylvania. After an extended period of hysterical laughter, my friend and I pulled ourselves together enough to think we could ask for directions in the bowling alley. However, a police car drove up beside us with three police officers inside—two in front, one in back. One officer said, without our having to say it, "You're lost. We'll lead you to the ramp for the interstate." That's exactly what they did. They drove alongside us and exited at the next off ramp, a little extra spirit help that was quite welcome! The rest of the way home we held deep conversation about the subject of discarnate souls, times we have experienced their presences, and how we felt about such encounters.

I studied Gram's teachings for the next three years, kept in touch with one of her authorized teachers, but felt no impulse to return to her home for a visit. Then, one day, I just felt like going to see her. When I told my friend, she said she had been having thoughts of going back, too. We called to make arrangements. The person who answered the phone howled with glee. She said, "They're all coming in. Gram put out a call to the spirit realms and everyone is showing up. Come." We had another wonderful weekend. Each time Gram taught, the lessons would go in just a bit deeper, sort of like the nail pounded into the wood with each blow of the hammer until it holds tight. This time the trip back to our homes was uneventful. I guess we had learned enough that we did not require the spirited shenanigans that abounded the first time we left Gram.

After the second intensive, I trusted Gram enough to call her to ask about the unusual experiences I was having. Predictably she would burst into laughter and joyfully finish my sentences. I always felt deeply reassured and understood by her. No one in my personal or professional life knew about the things that I was encountering. Gram knew.

Moreover, she could find the positive in absolutely anything that happened, no matter what it was.

One day I called to report that I had just had a huge "stopped time" incident while traveling to the North Carolina Outward Bound, NCOB, center in the Pisgah National Forest of North Carolina. I'd been tracking the mileage and the time to my destination with digital watch, car clock, and odometer. Sometime in the late afternoon, all three inexplicably ceased to function. I continued to drive up the rough mountain road, not knowing if I would reach the entrance to NCOB, wondering if I'd have to sleep in my car that night. Hours later, in the pitch dark, I reached the gates just as staff members were locking up. As I drove through, the clock, watch and odometer began to work again. It was ten p.m. I should have arrived no later than seven pm. No one else at the center had had such an experience. I asked. Something inexplicable, something big had happened. When I called her, Gram just laughed and said, "That's great! You went visiting. That's wonderful!" She did not tell me anything else—that was for me to understand when the time was right. Her response was sufficient. It calmed me, somehow normalized the abnormal.

Gram passed over on August 21, 2007. Her impact was worldwide, her contributions many and substantial. She taught tools for the creation of peace through truth and self-responsibility. Some will remember her for the Peace Elder Councils that gathered together elders from different tribal traditions. This was part of her vision, to help bring together some of the threads for the weaving of the great web of peace. She was deeply committed to preparing as many as she could for the times in which we now live. Her book, *Other Council Fires Were Here Before Ours*, coauthored with Jamie Sams, tells the history of humanity in story format, shows how humanity predictably goes astray, and speaks to what is required for humanity to get back on track. Gram loved unconditionally. She would not let anyone get away with negativity. She'd call you on it every time. Wisdom poured out of her naturally, always at just the right moment. When she had something to say, you absolutely stopped what you were doing and listened. Those she touched have uniquely woven the teachings she was destined to bring forward into the fiber of our lives and work so that the ancient wisdom will continue to flow onward.

THE PHYSICIAN

During the fall of 1991, I attended a lecture given by a well-dressed, handsome, charming, prominent physician. When it came time for questions, I challenged him. Unusual behavior for me, it was apparently attracting to him because he asked me out for a Coke at the end of the evening. The attraction between us was instantaneous and surprisingly magnetic. I immediately intuitively knew that whatever transpired between us would ultimately end in anger. Nonetheless curious, I plunged into what became an agonizing piece of soul retrieval. Curiosity overrode the not-so-subtle caution from my spirit team.

We dated only for a little over a month. For Christmas, he gave me a beautiful metal sculpture of Adam and Eve tempted by the serpent in the Garden of Eden. He was into symbolism. So was I. He lost interest in January. I was heartbroken. He told me I would be okay and that I would not see him again for a very, very long time. I wondered what he meant. The pain in my heart was unbearable until a for real earth angel cowboy came into my life to provide great distraction through wilderness romance, backpacking, rock climbing, candles, and intelligent conversation. Even so, the ache for the doctor lingered on for years.

Initially, I did not understand what drove the intensity I felt until I experienced vivid soul retrieval during a CranioSacral Somato-Emotional Release session. This is a form of deep yet subtle bodywork taught through the Upledger Institute. Spontaneously and without conscious bidding, I traveled backwards in time to a lifetime when I was a Sumerian priestess. The period was at the end of the Sumerian civilization as it cusped with ancient Egypt. I was consort to a handsome government official who just happened to be the present-day physician. He held a responsible position in the government and relied upon my insights with confidence. Our relationship was electric. One particular Egyptian priest detested me, wanted me out of the way because he thought I had too much influence with the official. One day while I was strolling alone beside a body of water, the Egyptian priest viciously attacked. He kicked my lower back with tremendous force. The attack left me paralyzed from the waist down. I lay helpless on the ground until rescued by people who took care of me until I died. The government official abandoned me completely. He never even came to say goodbye.

Late one night in 1992 A.D., the physician looked at me and asked, with puzzled consternation, "Who *are* you?" Twice his soul spoke directly through him to me: through this question, and again when he told me I would not see him again for a very, very long time. We never discussed the level of soul connection that we shared. While I had gained the capacity to see and hear the souls of others as a result of my wake-up experiences combined with Vision Quest and training by my two primary spiritual teachers, I knew that he'd dismiss what I heard come through him as some kind of nuttiness.

While I now understood a portion of our history together, that awareness did not ease the wrenching heartache of abandonment again by someone I loved at a soul level. Though I also retrieved information about other shared, enjoyable lifetimes, the short-lived reunion was to help me retrieve the part of my soul that had remained trapped in that ancient trauma. Because I did not listen to the initial warning the night we met at his lecture, I suffered again deep in my soul. I did not take very good care of my heart. It took years to let go of my obsessive thoughts of him. I came to understand the concept of obsession as the expression of unrequited love, and that the only antidote is love of oneself.

EGYPTIAN PRIEST

It turns out that my this-life father was the Egyptian priest who murdered me with that fateful, forceful kick. Let me tell you that when I finally realized this I was not a happy priestess! This revelation, in combination with other incidents, only fueled the anger I already felt toward him. It explained also some of the anxiety that surfaced whenever I had been alone with him during this lifetime. Would he hurt me again was not a conscious question, but certainly one that worked me from deep inside. Interestingly, my father traveled to Egypt toward the end of his life. He did not say much about the trip, but he surely remembered something because he carved his connection with Egypt. A fine woodworker, he disappeared into his basement workshop almost as soon as he returned home to carve and paint with perfection the head of King Tut, the full form of Anubis, and other figures from Egyptian history. The carvings are beautiful, and I consider them substantiating evidence to support the solved murder mystery. Of course, the carvings came to me by default after his death rather than to any other member of my family since no one else was interested in them.

Although my father passed over in 1982, I tenaciously refused to forgive him for various hurts, even when he came to me in spirit form nine years after his death so that we could continue our karmic healing. I had no awareness at that time about him as the priest murderer. He showed up in my bathroom at two a.m. while I was taking a shower. What nerve! I had just returned from my first workshop with Grandmother Twylah. During the long ride home's spirit discussions with my friend, I boldly drew the line and set absolute limits around spirit visitations: no discarnate souls in my bathroom. Period. I had the right to privacy. Sensing a presence, I peeked out of the shower curtain. Soap spewed from the soap dispenser that stood alongside the sink. The plunger was depressed. No physical person was in evidence. Once I noticed, the unseen force that pressed upon it released and the spewing stopped. Somehow, I just knew my father was present. I yelled bloody hell and cursed him out of the bathroom, told him not to come back until he had made amends with every family member for whatever unfinished business remained. I felt violated in that moment and thoroughly justified in my position. At the time, I did not understand that he was not seeing me in the buff. He was seeing me as the spirit I am.

Now I can say that it was very good that Dad came. He did visit family members over the next couple of weeks. I checked. The oddity of it all was that while I was furious, I was at the same time reluctant to call him out too strongly for fear of causing a heart attack in an already "dead" man. Dad died of a heart attack in 1982. His visit occurred in 1991. Such is the illogical power of long-term unfinished relational business. In spite of the anger I felt, I loved him. I did not want to hurt him. *We Don't Die*, the book by the well-known medium, George Anderson, helped me move beyond that irrational fear. Anderson shows, through story after story, how alive the departed actually are.

When I visited Turkey the end of November, 2006, the first requirement upon entering that beautiful and fascinating country was to write a letter of forgiveness to my father so that I could move on. My spirit guides told me that what would happen during the rest of the tour would be contingent upon this healing release. I had not known that this particular act of forgiveness was part of the travel package. Dad had done his part of the karmic clearing and I now had to do mine. I finally understood that it really served no purpose to hold onto anger that kept part of my soul bound in the long ago past. After taking a deep breath and clearing my mind, I wrote the letter. I did deserve to be free of this eons-old load. Forgiving my father made a huge difference. I immediately felt lighter. The trip went on to be a smashing success on all fronts. It was a journey through layers of time, civilizations, and religions, a journey filled to overflowing with unanticipated blessings and surprises.

That accomplished, I really thought we had finally cleared everything up. However, during 2009, my capacity to manifest work and money ground to a dead halt. I worked as hard as possible and with the most creative approaches and yet nothing I did was productive. A friend from Abadiania, Brazil, emailed to ask how I was. I told him I was in trouble, that I really needed help. He carried my prayer request to John of God and the Entities of the Casa de Dom Inacio. John of God is an extraordinarily clear healing medium who resides in Brazil. Through a process called incorporation, he vacates his body to allow one loving healing spirit at a time to serve those in attendance. Medium Joao — John of God — makes clear that he is not the healer. Repeatedly he states, "It is God who is the healer." Highly evolved healing spirits serve through him and the Casa de Dom Inacio, the spiritual center that is named for the famous healing saint, St. Ignatius.

Revelation with relief through the intervention initiated by John of God came almost overnight. Another spewing incident took place in the bathroom, this time involving hand lotion. A friend witnessed the physical incident. My father was involved somehow. There was no doubt about it. No one else has ever spewed in the bathroom but Dad. I actually heard my father say, "Oops. I forgot to remove the curses against prosperity that I placed upon you at the same time I kicked you. Sorry." I forgave Dad again, although to be honest I had a brief delayed-reaction hissy fit a few days later. My friend confessed that she had been skeptical about some of the physical events I'd told her about over the years. Eyewitness to the spewing lotion, she became a believer.

I'm still a bit incredulous about the whole thing. For years I had done my best to clear energetic blockages when I became aware of them. I believed that this was possible, that we can accomplish anything just by shifting our thoughts in a positive direction. While I still believe in the power of intentional thought, this experience provided yet another teaching. Stripped to the bone, I had begun to think that maybe it was just getting to be my time to move over to the other side. I began to ponder the adage, "You can't take it with you." Nothing made sense. Maybe it was just my time to exit. Thank God for the Brazilian friend who expressed concern, for the intervention through John of God by the Entities of the Casa de Dom Inacio, that my father 'fessed up. Thank goodness, too, for some preliminary work with two gifted healers and friends, Gabrielle Spencer and Selene. We had been removing attachments and ancient convoluted contracts that were intricately worded and imbedded. The work has been like negotiating a booby-trapped maze.

This experience deepened my understanding about the kinds of bizarre things that can wreak havoc in our lives. I have known for a long time about the power of curses and sorcery. While I do not endorse — ever — the use of such practices, I have met individuals and communities during my travels who wield esoteric knowledge on this subject and without compunction set such things in motion. I have striven to remove curses hurled upon me by those who know I know what they are doing. Sometimes I have needed help to get rid of them. This is Harry Potter School, for real. This is nasty business selfishly indulged in for purposes of power and control. Obviously, the cure is not always such a simple matter. I had prayed for help, asked for protection. Moreover, why would I ever suspect that my own this time loving birth father would have cast such a devious, disastrous curse upon me so very long ago? He was, however, not my father at that time. Not that that matters, mind you.

Curses and interference can be as simple as a thought shot out from one individual to another. I have met my share of psychically accomplished individuals, persons who are adept at moving energy to manifest what they want. During a trip to India in 2007, a high school principal invited me to make a presentation to his student body. Thrilled, I proceeded to prepare for the speech. However, the invitation seemed to dissolve into thin air, was never mentioned again even though it had seemed to be a solid request. Later, a person I had trusted casually told me that he had sent out a thought to stop the presentation because he was jealous.

Just think about the power of such thought. We already know that we can hurt by words and deeds. We need to be careful about our thoughts, as well. In the above instance, a psychically skilled, selfish individual deliberately projected a thought that affected me and other people without our knowing. Once given form even in the apparent privacy of one's own mind, thoughts become active. This is why we need to be careful. Recently I saw a photograph of a man purposefully sending a thought out from his mind. The camera caught the projected thought as it moved away from the man's head. The thought showed up as a golden oblong light. I assumed he was sending a positive thought, as dark usually shows up as dark. It is amazing to me that we can now "catch" such events scientifically.

One more story of this genre. Before I found out about the priest's curse that traveled with me through lifetimes to block prosperity, I decided to try something different to generate income. I joined a travel business that offers good discounts on airfares, hotels, vacation packages. It was a logical choice. I travel frequently as do many of my friends and colleagues. Enthusiastically, I happily sent emails out to people who might have interest. What happened in response was shocking. I began to receive emails and voicemails asking if I was okay, if something was wrong. The intent with which I had sent the emails in no way fit with the responses. Something else was at work behind the scenes. It turns out that "gloom and doom" was traveling along with my happy emails. What recipients of the emails responded to was the gloom and doom attachment rather than my good spiritedness. What helped to expose this nasty curse was the unanticipated expression of concern by friends about my well-being. Once identified, I was able to clear it with Gabrielle's help.

These lessons hold particular relevance for the field of psychotherapy. When patients are stuck in patterns that just don't seem to remit despite diligent engagement in psychotherapy using traditional modalities, the possibility that past life issues and other oddities are interfering should be considered and appropriate methods accessed to explore other times and places. I have come to the firm belief that much of what we encounter within ourselves is really the layered-in experiences accumulated through the longitudinal life of the soul. Once we begin to peel away the layers, we often find that something quite different is the root cause for the symptom. Symptoms that signal to us in our present day lives do their duty by serving as red flags to beckon us to time travel into the deeper regions of other lifetimes. When it is time, the flags do appear. Comforting is the considerable help that is cheering and helping us on from the "other side." Equal comfort comes from knowing that a solution to the presenting problem usually exists somewhere nearby. It is okay to ask for that assistance to appear. This would be right and valid use of energy.

One right after another three men appeared to prick the heartstrings of my soul. Shared with each man was a mutual experience of instant recognition along with a spoken sense that there were waters we mutually inhabited that were mystical, compelling and repelling simultaneously. A deep love for nature was in each instance part of the attraction. Our encounters were in some respects archetypal and transcended current space and time. We seemed to have peculiar interest in specific historical periods with distinct emphasis on matters of a spiritual inclination. The first was the physician. The second was the cowboy angel who rode in to rescue my broken heart and soothe my soul. The third was a rather psychologically complex, intellectually brilliant man who evoked memories of the many lives we had lived together in different civilizations.

This third man and I shared, with full consciousness, several remarkable simultaneous experiences. For instance, one day I retrieved snippets from a lifetime when he was a teacher in the Epicurean School of Philosophy in Greece. I had not studied philosophy this lifetime, knew nothing at all about Epicurean teachings, but that word came clearly into my mind during a CranioSacral Therapy session. En route that very same day to teach a philosophy class at a nearby college, my friend spontaneously changed the lecture he had prepared for that evening so that he could teach Epicurean concepts. He was shocked to learn the details of the soul retrieval I had experienced earlier. Amazing coincidences like this happened frequently between us. It was wonderful to share such consciousness even though we were not to be romantically involved. I knew I was not making things up because he, like my mother, validated my perceptions each step of the way. Validation always is rather satisfying.

When I returned from the white water canoe trip on the remote Dumoine River in northern Quebec, expanded from eight days in absolute wilderness, my reentry was to packed crowds at the height of the summer season at the shore. I slid into an abyss of deep grief. I went looking for my friend the academic only to learn that he was out of town biking in the Northwest. Bereft, I returned to my house. Shortly after, he called to ask what was wrong. I said, "Nothing. I'm fine." Not one to take no for an answer, he pressed until I confessed to being profoundly sad to be back in the "civilized" world. I asked why he called. He said he'd heard me crying and knew he needed to call. This is deep soul connection.

Pondering each of these intense relationships at dusk one evening while taking clothes down from the line out back of the house, I zeroed in on the connection with the cowboy. We shared a casual relationship. He did not live in state, just rode through once in a while. The thought I had was that the intimacy we shared had grown shallow. While we had great fun and conversations that were intellectually stimulating, something substantive was missing. At the peak of this thought, the streetlight across the street switched off. It was one of "those" moments. A message delivered to affirm the thought. Shocked, I went inside to get a grip, formulated a question, and shot it at the same streetlight that had turned back on. The light went out again. None of the other lights in the neighborhood behaved this way. They all stayed on. I stomped back into the house to find another way to ask the same question. Then I strode back out again onto the front porch and defiantly fired the reformulated query at the on-again streetlight. The result was the same. Then I heard—like a spoken thought inside my head—that I was to cease and desist with such relationships because we were not traveling the same paths.

Ruffled my feathers a bit, that did. It was okay for me to have such a thought, I thought—but to have the thought so thoroughly punctuated by the streetlights and the voice took it to a whole other level. I did what any woman so confronted would do: I called my friend the biking academic and said, "I'm not going to tell you what this is about. Just look outside your window and tell me what you see." He told me the streetlight across the street from his house blinked out. Obviously, this was a strong message, one I needed to heed. The next time the cowboy rode through, I told him that we needed to end things. He accepted what I said without question and we pleasantly went our separate ways. We had shared something enjoyable, but it was over.

That was my first encounter with what has become an ongoing relationship with what's called Street Lamp Interference, also referred to as SLI or SLIder psychic phenomenon. People who have these experiences sometimes know that more is involved than mere random occurrence. Princeton University's Engineering Anomalies Research Lab and Dr. Richard Wiseman at the University of Hertfordshire, England, have been engaged in research of SLI for years. The current thinking is that the subconscious mind is somehow involved, as well as charged emotional states and stress. That there's some kind of a charge going on is undisputed. Many who have SLI encounters also blow out light bulbs, computers, iPods, cell phones, appliances, and more. So something electric, some frequency is occurring between the individual and the object that's affected. One morning after an unanticipated spiritual initiation, my home computer conked out. Later that day I walked into a convenience store and the electronic cash register blew. Astonished, I paid for some items and left. I have not been able to own a walkman, the older equivalent of today's iPod, after shorting out six units in a row. The store took them back, no questions asked. I was grateful.

Personally, I believe that my Divine Self—what many call Higher Self—spirit guides, and teachers have something to do with this. While sometimes stress or emotional overload can be a trigger for the lights to go out, I have more often felt the loving presence of guidance and protection. Sometimes when I'm lost, the lights will go on like runway lights to show me the way. When I must drive through not-so-safe areas, the lights provide comforting reassurance. Often when returning from a long trip, the lights blink out as I am on final approach to my home. Clearly. I have my own personal escort service! The SLI events make me giggle. I know I am not alone.

There are interesting websites to explore this subject further. Typing in the keywords street light phenomenon will bring up a list of sites. Ask.com site guide Steve Wagner provides easy links to some research sites along with a blog for experiencers. It is a bit of a challenge to give you these stories in a straight line and, sometimes, with a straight face. There is so much to share. I am definitely not writing this book all by myself. In fact, the book writes itself when my fingers connect with the keyboard of my computer.

Let us turn back now to the subject of soul partnerships. Although emotionally charged encounters, the soul retrievals that resulted from the soul reunions really gave me something substantive to work with. I do not take soul retrieval lightly. It is not a game, not an indulgence. Each retrieval event comes forward for specific reasons. Usually healing is involved, perhaps a reworking of a relational pattern, maybe a teaching. With the cowboy and the biking academic, both were friends from long ago who showed up at just the right time for different reasons. I needed to feel desirable after the heartbreak with the physician. The cowboy helped me with that. That he and I are soul-connected is indisputable because, years later, we continue to tag-team one of his family members with "coincidental" phone calls only moments apart. She's part of our soul group, too, and knows it. The moments shared with the academic expanded my appreciation for how souls travel together through time in such memorable ways. He validated my recall. I validated his. Conscious, he was also able to discuss the state of his soul. We both knew we had restorative soul work to do and discussed that fact. A big learning has been that heartfelt soul reconnects might not be for rekindling an ancient romance. Such reunions can be confusing, sometimes addicting in their intensity—as in the case of the physician. It takes a bit of sorting out to figure out the reason for the reconnect. While no longer in contact with any of them, I respect all three men for their fine contributions toward making this world a better place. Our limited time together was productive.

One thing is certain. Patterns in need of redress from this lifetime and other lifetimes keep on coming until the unfinished business is resolved. White Waters has pointedly said, "We are our own life's work. We are here to heal our soul." The soul retrievals have been fascinating, illuminating, sometimes arduous, and always worthwhile. They have even prompted exploration of ancient civilizations, religious and spiritual belief systems. All this has been soul level work. When I look at the places soul restoration has taken me, I am truly in awe.

PART TWO
DIVE DEEPER

1992 was a remarkable year of change. I was divorced after twenty years of marriage. I graduated from a three-year post-masters clinical psychotherapy program. With marital home sold as part of the divorce, I purchased a new home. I went into private practice. With all this change, I was ripe for the pickings for a ten-day Jungian retreat in Oaxaca, Mexico, during Day of the Dead festivities.

Day of the Dead celebrations, unique to Mexico, have evolved from ancient indigenous traditions to honor the souls of departed loved ones during the time of the year when the veils between worlds are thin. Altars in each home are colorfully laden with flowers, fruits, and nuts. Special foods are prepared, including beautifully decorated breads and silver-beaded sugar skulls. Cemeteries are bursting with flowers of riotous hues. Boom boxes blare ear-shattering music from atop the graves of the deceased. Sobbing and laughter are heard everywhere. Beginning on All Saints Day, November 1, this is a time of ceremonial respect for visiting other side relatives that concludes ten days later as adults and children line dance through the countryside in costumes. Day of the Dead, with its reverence and celebration of the deceased, is vastly different from the fear-based Halloween celebrated in the United States.

Shortly before traveling to Oaxaca, I had a graduation dream. It was clear as clear could be. Once in Oaxaca I dreamed that I dove into a very deep pool. The sense that I had entered into a deeper stratum of self-work proved true. During the ten days, we had the opportunity to experience firsthand the exceptional healing gifts of some of the local curanderos. Spirit-guided healers, each one had a unique way of working. I was fortunate to spend time with each one.

The recommendations given were just perfect. It was as though a master treatment plan was in place so that each visit with a curandero supported the overall effort. One curandero, Guillermo, wanted to give me a particular Mother Mary blessing but did not because he did not seem to trust the interpreter. He was quite specific that I receive massage up rather than down my spine when I returned home. Following his advice, I began two years of frequent CranioSacral Therapy and massage sessions with a local practitioner. This form of light-touch energy healing helped me to access my body's inner wisdom, which in turn allowed clearings called "releases" to occur. The retrievals—for the most part vivid soul retrievals—uncannily interfaced with physical symptoms, events, and people in my current life. Opened up in this way through the bodywork, deeper levels of resolution became possible. An unforeseen benefit was the elimination of respiratory ailments that had previously caused me to lose a month of work each year.

Juana, a Zapotec healer whose gifts drew people from around the world to her humble family compound, was the highlight for me. This tiny wiry woman was intense, so intense that some men were skittish in her presence. The notion that she was considered a witch struck fear into the hearts of the male members of our group, by their own admission. But we women just loved her. Two others and I got up very early one morning to hike the cart trail from the retreat center to her home. We waited for hours for Juana while she and her family performed their daily chores. The men moved wheelbarrow upon wheelbarrow of animal and human excrement to an unseen destination. Juana plied those of us who awaited her ministration with exceptionally delicious coffee and pastries. Then it came time for her to work.

The long period of waiting had activated a deep anxiety within me. When it was my turn to lie down on the healing mat, I was petrified. Juana read me right. She placed her right arm right down the center of the front of my upper body from my neck to my abdomen and ran calming energy to calm me. Relaxed, I sank into a state of bliss. Then she grabbed my throat. That was a bit of a surprise, but I was so content that I thought, "Well, if she wants to kill me it's okay." We traveled to an ancient place and time where I heard a loving male voice say, "It was not your fault." I did not understand until later what that meant—it had to do with the fall of Atlantis—but I surely did feel less burdened. Then Juana stuffed healing leaves in my underwear and spat alcohol all over me to complete the limpia, the spiritual cleansing.

Prior to visiting the fifth and final curandero, a woman named Concepcion, I sobbed uncontrollably and without context from the deepest depth of my soul for a solid twenty-four hours. I looked forward to sitting with her and the spirits that she channeled. Everyone just raved about her. The session did not at all turn out the way I had hoped. It did not feel like a love bath. She did not sing praises to me. It was a brief, direct confrontation. She told me that I had a very sick soul. Devastated and terribly ashamed, I declined to see her again. She said that I needed to heal my heart. For years afterwards, I could not get those words out of my mind. Even though what was said so bluntly proved to be true, the experience was extremely traumatizing. It took years to recover as I unraveled the story behind that statement. I am not going to sit in judgment of her or of myself. Harsh as the event was, perhaps I needed that shock to get moving. I am not going to worry about it any longer because I have moved through hell to heal.

CURE FOR SMOKING

Guillermo the curandero had wanted to give me a Mother Mary prayer. I grew up in the Methodist Church, not the Catholic Church. Mary was Catholic. Protestant church brings Mary out for Christmas and again at Easter. The rest of the year, it is as though she does not exist. Consequently, I did not know to call upon her for healing.

For many years, I had unsuccessfully tried to stop smoking. There were long periods of abstinence but no permanent extinction of the habit. Suddenly, in 1993, each time I lit up I'd feel immobilized, dizzy, nauseated to the extreme, and then would have to put the cigarette out. I couldn't have smoked. It was impossible. Somehow, I just knew that Mother Mary was present to help me. I did not see her. I did not hear her. I had no known prior experience with her yet I just knew she was there and that she was helping me. The cure, a form of inter-dimensional aversion therapy, has been lasting. Mother Mary literally reached through the veils to help me. My mother died in 1987 from metastatic lung cancer caused by a lifetime of heavy smoking. I believe that Mary saved me from a similar fate.

Despite the 1985 heart-healing experience with my mother and Mother Mary's cure of my smoking addiction in 1993, I apparently needed further healing. Call it thought field transfer, call it environmental modeling, call it what you like, the reason I even smoked in the first place remained unanswered. Full understanding came during two days of training in a psychotherapeutic method called EMDR, the acronym for Eye Movement Desensitization Reprocessing. This is a powerful healing modality developed by Francine Shapiro, Ph.D., for her work with Vietnam veterans suffering from Post-Traumatic Stress Disorder. Deep reaching, this total sensory/cognitive method unlocked the secret behind the addictive behavior even though I had chosen a seemingly unrelated incident from kindergarten to work on, one that had repeatedly come into my consciousness since childhood for no apparent reason. I had no intent going into the session to receive more healing related to my mother and our addiction to cigarettes.

Five years old, I was just back to Kindergarten after having had my tonsils and adenoids removed. Full of the surgical experience, I returned to school with the puppet the hospital staff gave me. Eager to tell all after a week of painful post-surgical silence, I was so chatty that the teacher separated me from the rest of the class. She put me in a punishment chair away from my classmates. The EMDR kicked in at this point, showed me how traumatic to my innately effervescent innocent self the separation from my classmates was. I saw that after this event I began to shut down.

I lost self-confidence. Eventually, one event piled on top of the other and I avoided speaking at all in the classroom. I did not conquer this fear of speaking until my second year of graduate school—twenty-three years later. I loved my Kindergarten teacher. I do not think she intended to wound my spirit. The session really helped make sense of a critical childhood event that had been perplexing in its periodic tweaking of my memory, no explanation given. How very tender is the heart of the child.

The EMDR next propelled me straight out of the Kindergarten classroom into a state of co-conscious awareness of my self, as spirit, watching my mother smoke during her pregnancy with me. I observed from outside the physical body that I was to merge with at birth. I saw and smelled my mother smoking. Spirit me interpreted that she did not care enough to stop smoking to take proper care of the little body growing inside her. Next came a moment of epiphany. In a flash of insight, I understood why I'd begun to smoke when I became a teenager: it was my attempt to understand why my mother smoked. During the EMDR session, I complained to the team that was working with me about smelling cigarette smoke in the room. Irritated, I asked why the workshop leaders would ever permit anyone to smoke in the conference room. The next day, when my session was completed, the team said that no one had been smoking in the training room. Only I smelled cigarette smoke. The smell of smoke was in my memory.

EMDR and other psychotherapeutic modalities that have emerged over the past twenty years have proven to be excellent vehicles to get at what's really cooking below the surface. My experience demonstrated the phenomenon called chaining: certain events connecting together like links of chain. In that instance, the entry point of the hurt caused by the kindergarten teacher/mother figure helped me to access the original pre-natal hurt by my birth mother. Deep lasting healing requires getting to the original injury and, as in good wound care, cleaning the pus out from the point of origin. The rebirth experience triggered during Dr. Whitfield's workshop had gifted me threefold. I learned about the consciousness of the spirit that was about to be born, that what is experienced during this gestational time is recorded and has lasting impact throughout one's life. The rift between my mother and me from lack of birth bonding acknowledged and partially healed, Mother Mary's divine intervention cured me of the physical smoking addiction. The waving red flag school memory guided me to complete this particular body of work.

My soul was driving this process. All that was required was that I follow the clues. I had not consciously called any of the healing experiences forward. The healings with my mother and then with my father flowed seamlessly into the development of a surprising relationship with Mother Mary. The Great Mother, Queen of Heaven, Mother to All, Supreme Goddess, Mother of Many Names stepped forward to help me heal my wounded soul. Her intervention was proof of her availability to every one of us, regardless of our religious or spiritual affiliation. Grateful, I gave my heart to Mary and vowed to serve The Mother from that time forward.

IMMACULATE CONCEPTION

In July 1994, I drove through upstate New York, once again on my way to grown-up camp in northern Ontario, Canada, this time to co-lead a seven-day women's wilderness canoe trip. My snazzy tan and white Chevy Blazer and I headed towards yet another great adventure. I sang "Silent Night" in sync with a favorite Christmas carol tape after having listened to Deepak Chopra's excellent audio cassette, *Magical Mind, Magical Body*. Dr. Chopra's discussion about quantum physics in relation to health was intriguing. I had not previously considered the idea that the body is not the solid mass that we believe it to be, that there is actually space between the cells. Through the process of cellular shedding and the creation of new cells, our bodies are continually renewed. This same shedding process offers opportunities to effect changes in the body.

Deep in contemplation, I was excited to learn about the potential for physical renewal through the purposeful shifting of thought. In this place of delicious consideration, something happened. The quantum physics of my mind shifted to allow a startling idea to enter. In a moment of transcendence, I understood in my bones the true meaning of the Immaculate Conception. The insight simply dropped in and settled itself within me. With unprecedented clarity, without prior deliberation, I just absolutely understood that every single one of us *is* the Immaculate Conception. We are pure spirit, innocent gifts from God who come down to enter into the physical body created by our parents to hold us. Awestruck by this revelation, I saw the whole process. We spiral down from Godhead to enter into the container called body. We are anchored in the body by the soul that is created at the moment of birth. We remain in the physical body until the physical life is complete and then we lift up and out of the physical body at the moment of death. We are spirit that comes and goes. We are not the body. The body is the sacred temple that holds us while we are here. I was stunned. This idea made more sense than did anything I ever heard in church. The concept of original sin dissolved. We are not bad. We are not born automatically tainted. We are beautiful emanations come down from God.

Just in case I had any doubt about what happened during that car ride, and I did not, Mother Mary sent a gift through a friend who had spent her summer in Greece. When I returned home from the wilderness adventure, my friend presented me with a beautiful icon of Mary holding baby Jesus.

You need to understand that I did not have any conceptual framework for these experiences. Discussions about the Immaculate

Conception, the world of saints and of Mary apparitions were just not part of my religious upbringing. Previously I had known and felt the presence of God only while singing hymns. I had despaired of finding what I intuitively knew existed. I could not find "it" with any consistency in church. There were not even words to describe what I was looking for. I just knew there was more than what was taught in Sunday school or from the pulpit.

Over the next few years, I would better understand the dance between spirit, soul, and body. Our spirit hovers close to the body until the time of actual birth. Then, the soul manifests instantaneously to anchor our spirit in the physical body. We live our lives. When we have completed the reasons for incarnating, the body dies. As soul and spirit, we cross back over into the spiritual realms at the time of death for more healing and learning. When it is time for another round of Earth School, the soul and spirit return together. The returning soul does not come back identical to how it was when it left the body at the end of the prior incarnation. This is because of the healing and teachings it has received during the out-of-body time. Each re-entry into the physical body produces another layer of soul around our spirit. The soul carries the load of the karmic, unfinished business from each time of embodiment. When all debts—unfinished business—are satisfactorily concluded, the spirit is set free from the wheel of karma. Further need for incarnation becomes unnecessary and the housing called soul dissolves. The spirit then has the choice to continue to serve humanity as bodhisattva, like White Waters, or to move on.

Many authors have written on matters pertaining to soul. I especially appreciate the books authored by Brazil's most famous and highly respected medium, Francisco Candido Xavier. Nicknamed Chico, his life was devoted to bringing through messages about life in the spiritual realms. A good place to begin is with the book, *Nosso Lar*, which is the first in a collection of teachings told in story form by the spirit named Andre Luis. The material in Xavier's books has consistently corroborated and expanded what I have been learning through experience. Chico Xavier's books are excellent in helping people to understand the interface between the physical and spiritual realms, what happens when we "die," where we go and what we do when we are on the other side.

SOUL RECOGNITION

One of my clients studied at the Barbara Brennan School of Energy Healing. Barbara Brennan is a NASA physicist who left that field to teach energy healing. Students come from all over the world to learn the intense four-year curriculum taught at her school. In 1994, this particular client brought information about a process called Soul Recognition that was offered through an organization named Soul Support Systems. I kept the literature but did nothing with it, just tucked it away. About the same time, bedtime started to become rather interesting. Each night when I climbed into bed a most beautiful, pulsing, vibrant blue light enveloped me. Visible to my open eyes, the light would appear from out of nowhere. As the light enfolded then entered me, a deep comfort radiated through my body accompanied by deep inner tingling from head to toe. There was nothing whatsoever disturbing about this. I somehow knew just to accept the gift even though its source was unknown. I went to bed every night for many months in this beautiful energy.

Then I began to receive unusual messages on my voicemail. They were beeps, like some kind of a Morse code. The messages appeared on the machine when I was thinking, reading, talking with someone about or attending seminars whose subject was soul and spirit. I could be in the house, pick up the phone and find a message even though the phone had never rung. For instance, one day my stockbroker was visiting. We wound up discussing spiritual matters while sitting in the kitchen where the phone was located. The phone never rang. The ringer was on. After he left, I went to make a call and found yet another beep-bop-boop message waiting.

For some reason the mysterious messages just filled my heart with joy. My friends did not believe me when I told them what had been happening. A close friend, also a colleague, called one day to tell me of her sincere concern for my mental health. She was positive that the messages were electronic messages from a telemarketing company. I listened to her concern for my well-being with appreciation, but, in my bones, I knew something beautiful was happening even though others and I did not understand it. After we hung up, another message was waiting, a message just like the others. I called her back. She laughed and said, "Don't even tell me!" We had a good chuckle together at the mystery of it all.

Eventually I learned that Flo Aeveia Magdalena, teacher of the Soul Recognition process, would be in my area to teach the Soul Recognition Facilitator work. Succumbing, for I admit to having had a dug-in unfathomable resistance to attending that workshop, I put the course registration check in the mail. Immediately the mysterious calls stopped. They just plain stopped. A great amount of effort evidently had gone into getting me into the Soul Recognition cattle chute. Whoever had been doing these things—the bedtime blue light specials and the answering machine beep-bop-boops—was taking a well-deserved break. I am certain they yelled, "Glory Hallelujah!" They probably also muttered something like, "Boy, what a stubborn little doggie she is."

The soul remembering process as taught to Flo Aeveia Magdalena by Mary Magdalene was incredible. I experienced soul retrieval that included bells, whistles, visible balls of spirit dancing on the ceiling, and I saw and heard it all. It was life changing. I really did feel different from the inside out. Again that my destiny was intertwined with Mary was made evident, this time by Flo Aeveia Magdalena when she autographed the title page of her book, *I Remember Union, The Story of Mary Magdalena*, this way: "May you work Mary's journey with her and bring the silence of the truth with you wherever you go, always remembering that the truth releases its own story." I had no idea what a prophetic statement this would prove to be. All I knew was that Mary unconditionally loved me, had healed me, and that I had devoted my life to her the year before.

By now my understanding was that no human love could ever truly satisfy my and others' deep yearning for mother and father love. My belief is that the deep sense of loss we seek to soothe comes from the experience of dropping down from the holy womb of Original Creation, called The Absolute by Flo Aeveia, to take on human form. We feel ourselves to be separate from our true home even though this is not exactly the case. Once we enter life in the physical plane, we lapse into a state of forgetfulness. We disremember our connection with Source. We forget how unconditionally loved we are. We forget how to make contact with Source. This, to me, is the original separation anxiety. Soul Recognition work is a wonderful gift to help us to remember. Think about it this way. Bumblebees are devoted to their queen. They become highly anxious when away from her. At the end of their day's work, they literally make a beeline back to the hive where they form a huge mass around her. They snuggle in as close as they can. They know the way. They know how to go home. We, the forgetters, need nudges.

Thank goodness for the persistence of The Ones With No Names (TOWNN). I learned about them during Soul Recognition. An off-planet bodhisattva consciousness that had come in closer to our planet to stimulate the awakening of sleepy souls, they were the blue lights who had been visiting me at bedtime and leaving the voicemail messages. TOWNN was to make another particularly memorable voicemail appearance on a Saturday a couple of months later.

I was having one of those days. The hanging door in the den was off its track. It refused to go back into place. I struggled with it for quite a while. The more I struggled, the unhappier I became. All right, so I cursed a blue streak in frustration. I decided to take a break, make a cup of tea, and calm myself down. While waiting for the water to boil I picked up the phone to make a call. A voicemail message was waiting, so I checked to see who had called. This voicemail was twenty minutes long! My voicemail system did not work that way—thirty seconds per message was the outer limit. As I listened to the familiar sound of beep-bop-boops, my body and mind began to relax. A sense of joy bubbled back up. I laughed with gratitude that my friends from "upstairs" had dialed in to say they love me.

Next, I sat down with the cup of tea and looked out the den windows into the lush green backyard. Without fanfare, the Two-Squirrel Revue appeared on top of the fence. Two fantastic plump gray squirrels performed a Punch and Judy type show. They fake-boxed with each other, then would disappear down the other side of the fence only to pop up again to re-enact their fake boxing routine. They did this repeatedly. They were hilarious. Then they simultaneously jumped onto the tree branch that hung above the fence. Hanging upside down side by side, they swung back and forth by their hind legs for a few moments. Any residual irritation I had dissolved with their riotous antics. Finally, they chased each other up into the higher branches. It was spring. The green buds were taking form. Snack time! My furry friends dined as if they were enjoying the finest caviar. To finish the show, a Scarlet Tanager, a rare bird to see, flew into the same tree and sat a while. Scarlet Tanagers were one of my mother's favorite birds. I knew she had come to cheer me up. How could I go wrong with such a great support team?

One final treat to share from the Soul Support Systems' goodie bag is a concept called "Sunlight on Water." Shimmering golden light where the rays of sunlight hit the water is what we look like, is what it looks like when Heaven and Earth meet. It is a blinding, brilliant, sparkling, dancing, joyful golden light. We are so beautiful.

Fast forward now to April 2009, the Big Island of Hawaii. Driving along the coast the first evening, I just could not keep my eyes off the shimmer of gold on the ocean where the rays of the late afternoon sun touched the water. It was magical, a stunning display that all of a sudden had me exclaiming, "Oh, that's Sunlight on Water!" I was so happy. The same phenomenon occurred the next afternoon. That evening while leafing through an island vacation guide, I saw a dolphin swim boat called Sunlight on Water. Then the phone rang. The arrangements for our deep-water dolphin swim had fallen through. The woman on the phone provided names for some reputable dolphin swim companies to contact. She particularly recommended Sunlight on Water. Laughing, I called the number and, sure enough, the owners knew Flo Aeveia Magdalena and the Soul Recognition work. Without doubt, we are in the hands of loving angels.

The years between 1994 and 1997 were a time of seasoning, deepening, and integration. Life was interesting and fulfilling. Then in late spring of 1997, I felt compelled to attend the Wesak Festival held near Mt. Shasta, California. I knew it was important to go even though I knew no one attending and had no real idea of what would happen there. Thousands of spiritually minded people would gather to celebrate Buddha's birth and life. Wesak festivals, I later learned, are a worldwide Buddhist tradition.

I had a lucid dream visitation beforehand. The pleasant face of an aristocratic man appeared. He was slender, proper, well dressed, and of European nobility. He remained long enough that I would not forget his face. Rather irreverently I thought, "Hmm, he's not the kind of guy you'd roll around in the grass with. He wouldn't want to get all muddied up." Imagine my surprise at finding his photo at the St. Germain Foundation in Mt. Shasta. As soon as I checked into the motel, I headed to the little white building that seemed to be insisting that I come have a look-see. There I learned that the man in my dreams was St. Germain, a fact that still meant nothing to me. Soon enough, I learned that he is a well-loved Ascended Master, one of those graduated souls I mentioned earlier. He lived more than three hundred years during his last physical lifetime. There are diaries and documents that support the fact that he really existed. Mt. Shasta, I learned, is a primary spiritual retreat for St. Germain. His energy overlights the spiritually charged higher dimensional region. The dream initiated an ongoing delightful relationship with this hard-working master, and provided the letter of introduction to many other masters, as well.

A small group of folks from California quickly befriended me. One of the members of the group adopted me while we waited in line for the restroom. They were a fun, interesting little community, definitely different from people I knew back home. They were quite elemental — elfin and fairy-like. Eleven of us skipped class after lunch on the second day of the weekend festival to meditate at a humble, sweet garden called "Mary's Garden." Situated in the center of Mt. Shasta in the middle of a residential neighborhood, the garden contained a tinkling, three-tiered tiny waterfall. As we gathered, we noticed a woman quietly meditating on a bench. We invited her to join our group. After the meditation, the woman went to her car. She returned with beautiful eight by ten color photos of Mother Mary that she then presented to each of us. The photos were of a painting that hangs in an early Coptic church in El Zeitoun,

Egypt. This was to be the beginning of an enduring relationship with Sandy.

Wanting to immerse again in the earthy simplicity of Mary's Garden, I attempted to return there the next day. I could not find it, which I found strange. The City of Mt. Shasta is not that large. I felt as though someone or something was preventing me from going there. Instead, I somehow wound up at a breakfront of trees at a site just on the edge of town. Behind the tall cedars was gruesome evidence of a tree massacre. The trees still standing were in a state of mourning amid the debris of their chopped down relatives. There was a terrible grief on that land. By the time I left the wounded area, night had fallen. The next day was my last day in Mt. Shasta. Trying again, this time I found the garden with ease. To my astonishment, most of my new meditation friends and some folks I did not know were at the site, waiting. We came together for a blessing of the little waterfall. Afterwards, a minister from Hawaii, new to the gathering, went to his car. He returned with a photo of Mary for me. The photo was a copy of the rainbow-colored image of Mother Mary that had appeared on December 23, 1996 on the side of a building in the financial district of Clearwater, Florida. I recalled having seen this image on national news.

Mary kept making her presence known. Soon after Wesak, a good friend gave me her copy of *Alone of All Her Sex*, a book about Mother Mary. Next, I noticed an announcement for the start up of Wednesday noon Rosary prayers at a local parish. I attended the first three meetings because it seemed important to be there. Each week I watched the men attempt to draw the women into taking on a leadership role. Each week I watched the women shrink from the offer, evidently preferring to remain passive participants. I wanted to yell to the women, "Get up there and just do it! Mary wants you to take the baton. You can do it!" I don't know the outcome, but the offer by the men surely seemed to be a timely gesture in a disturbed world where the feminine needs to rise up to take its proper place, a balanced place, alongside the masculine.

The Wesak Festival introduced me to the world of Ascended Masters, Archangels, and other divine beings. This was a quantum leap from the wonderfully intimate coterie of personal spiritual teachers that I had so far been fortunate to have step forward to help me. Through connections made at Wesak, I entered into a period of intense international travel for sacred purpose with groups primarily led by Dr. Norma Milanovich of Athena Leadership Center. Between 1997 and 2002, I traveled to Hawaii, Egypt, the Amazon of Brazil and Peru, Galapagos, Australia, New Zealand, Tibet, Outer Mongolia, Spain, Portugal, France, Jordan, Cyprus, and Malta. Most trips included spontaneous soul retrieval experiences—personal as well as collective. The growth spurt for me was phenomenal.

BROKEN LEG

The unraveling of yet another story began in the office of my psychotherapist back in the late 1980's. I asked her to hypnotize me so that I could resolve something from about age eight. I did not know why that age was significant but it was frequently on my mind. She induced me into a trance state, but I didn't stay there long. The pain in my head was so severe that I screamed myself right out of trance. We were both quite shaken; she more than myself, I think. We never ventured there again.

After returning from the 1992 Mexico trip, I upheld my agreement to Guillermo to obtain massage therapy. I had carried the business card of a local practitioner in my wallet for two years but had not attempted to contact her. It was time. At the beginning of our first session, she asked what the matter was with my right leg. I said, "Nothing." She persisted in questioning about that leg. I told her that I broke my left leg the summer before my eighth birthday when I fell from monkey bars at the park across from the lake where I took swimming lessons. Soaking wet, wearing my Mickey Mouse Fan Club red moccasins and matching red suede purse, I apparently slipped from the bars. I came to when the local rescue squad folks waved smelling salts below my nostrils. Next was the ambulance ride to the hospital where my left leg was painfully yanked back into place and casted. Perhaps something about the right leg stood out due to overuse of it during the time of healing. The therapist and I went on to clear an odd tingling sensation that had recently begun to radiate across the occipital region of the back of my head after a fall while skiing. I had seen three doctors about the odd sensation but none thought anything was abnormal. To my amazement, what I realized during the bodywork was that I had suffered a concussion during the fall from the monkey bars. That explained why I had no recall of the accident until brought back to consciousness by the rescue squad. The persistent tingling left with this remembrance.

In 1997, I met a medicine man during a Peace Elder Council organized by Grandmother Twylah Nitsch and the Wolf Clan Teaching Lodge. He invited me back to his home at the end of the event. Curious, I went. He offered to do some healing work on me. Shortly after the session began, my right leg started to feel quite strange. Then I went into a serious state of panic because my right leg felt completely dead. It was dead. I could not move it, could not feel it. Scared, I insisted that we immediately end the session. The experience was frightening. I didn't know what this was about but I knew it was important.

Once back home I asked a friend and colleague, another Barbara Brennan student, to help me figure the leg thing out. She was someone I knew well and trusted completely. The resolution came quickly. As we followed the story of the fall from the monkey bars, I instantaneously catapulted into a City of Light. I knew this place. I was happy to be home in the spiritual realms with precious friends and family. After a brief reunion, someone indicated that it was time to return to my physical body. I did not want to go back, but staying was not an option. Before traveling back down the tube of light, someone taught me how to reconnect with my spiritual family anytime I chose. I was to stand in the woods that surrounded my home, hold my arms tight to the sides of my body, and flap my hands as though I was flying. The result would be instant reunion. Instructions delivered, I returned to my body at warp speed. Well, this was new news. I had had a Near Death Experience. It had taken almost ten years to bring this story to the surface. I could not have been more surprised. The right leg was the key to accessing this story. By the way, the hand flapping technique worked quite well. I can't tell you anything about what happened but I surely do remember standing many times at a particular spot in the backyard and flapping my hands.

The storylines that run through each of our lives can be surprising. By following the clues, by living our stories, where we can go and what we can learn is incredible. White Waters wisely taught that the true learning comes from going deep inside, that everything we need to know is contained within.

On October 13, 1999, while driving south from New Hampshire on Interstate 95 after attending funeral services for my eldest brother, I began to notice unusual phenomena in the sky near Boston. It was daytime. For the first time I saw a dark "ship" in the sky. It was cloudlike, a perfectly rounded, dark charcoal gray, layered, lenticular formation, definitely not an ordinary cloud. Instinctively I knew that this "ship" was a manifestation of the forces of darkness—energies that have turned away from love and that some would term evil. The dark spirit ones are those who have forgotten how to love, who seek to dominate the masses through manipulation and control. Shaken deeply by this recognition, my heart dropped into my stomach. Then I heard a strong male voice, the voice I have come to know as that of Archangel Gabriel, say, "Armageddon has begun."

I knew he spoke the truth. Traveling southbound, the entire air corridor from Boston to New Jersey abounded with a legion of white cloud formations. Having seen these before, I knew they were the "ships" of the spiritual Forces of Light. The good news was that the "good guys" had amassed in great numbers that day. These often rainbow-hued distinctive formations provide physical demonstration of the presence of the Hierarchy of Light: God's messengers and Warriors of Light, Archangels, Angels, Ascended Masters, including Jesus, Mary, Mary Magdalene, St. Germain, Buddha and so many more, here to assist us through this tumultuous time, the physicality of their presence providing a profound source of comfort to those of us who are aware of them.

Later that day I retrieved a spiritual teacher from the airport in Philadelphia. I told him what I had heard and witnessed and that the long-prophesied great battle had begun. He commented that it made sense given that October 13 is the anniversary date for the Fatima prophecies. Even though I would visit Fatima in November, I did not know the specifics of these particular prophecies. My framework for prophecy had so far come primarily from indigenous teachings, particularly Grandmother Twylah's.

Dr. Norma Milanovich led our large group on a pilgrimage from Fatima, Portugal, to Lourdes, France, during November, 1999. Fatima is the site where Mary appeared six times to three young cousins beginning on May 13, 1917. She came to them on the thirteenth day of the month over a period of six months. Her final visitation was on October 13, 1917. Announcing herself as "The Lady of the Rosary," Mary gave three prophetic messages that she requested be delivered to the Vatican. Two of the children, Francisco and Jacinta, died soon after from the Spanish flu that killed millions beginning in 1918. Lucia, the third, went on to become a Carmelite nun. She was the child who recorded Mary's messages. Apparently, there was great resistance by the Vatican to these messages. The transfer process, accomplished in great secrecy, took many years. Sister Lucia died at the age of ninety-seven on February 13, 2005.

The first two message visions graphically depicted hell and the saving of souls from hell through prayer and conversion, with special attention given by the Holy Mother to the importance of the consecration of Russia. She told the children that without the consecration of Russia, the world would be plunged into awful war and devastation. The text of the third vision continues to be the subject of noteworthy controversy. Persons within and outside the Catholic Church have expressed concern that the entirety of the third prophecy has not yet been fully disclosed. They believe there is more to the prophecy than a cataclysmic event on a mountaintop where possibly a Pope and other religious leaders will die somehow after they pass through a ruined large city, its streets strewn with the bodies of untold numbers of dead.

During our visit at Fatima, the sky filled with rainbows and the image of Mother Mary. Our group then proceeded toward Lourdes by bus. We traveled a portion of the ancient pilgrimage route called the Way of St. James, known also as the Camino de Santiago. This was the route of St. James' ministry. Another highlight was our visit to Bom Jesus do Monte, a pilgrimage site located near Braga, Portugal. Bom Jesus is famous for its stunning architecture and dramatic presentation of the Stations of the Cross. While there, we watched streams of white light cascade from the sky all the way down onto the pavement. Simultaneously a clear image of Mary appeared as a cloud formation in the sky. More signs in the sky!

INQUISITION

Crossing over into Spain from Portugal, I unexpectedly found myself challenged by a sudden-onset respiratory condition. The nostril irritating strong smell of burning wood started the moment we entered Spain. Why it was happening was a puzzle. No one else reported the bothersome smell. I had no answer until the night we stayed in the medieval city of Leon. Feverish and unable to eat, I soaked in the bathtub and asked for understanding from my Divine Self and Spirit Guides. The information came in a vision.

Apparently, I was reliving my burning at the stake by the Inquisition for helping people with my knowledge of herbal remedies, knowledge passed down by the women of my lineage. While of favored birth, this social status made no difference in the eyes of the inquisitors. My children and mother were forced to watch me burn. The smell of burning wood, respiratory distress, and fever were part of the physical soul retrieval. Years before I had processed the burning both cognitively and emotionally, but not on a physical level. Before that moment, I had not known the specific location. I also had not known that my children and my mother were forced to watch me burn. During the vision, I saw that my soul shot straight up out of my body during the event, with the consequence that I had little recall of the actual experience. The physical reliving of my death allowed for the retrieval of the soul fragments that had lingered in the city of Leon, Spain, and in my soul body since the time of that death.

I was not the only one reliving trauma through the body. Some of my colleagues' bodies displayed graphic evidence of whiplash; others, of rope burns around their necks from being dragged behind carts; still others, angry-looking lesions that erupted to tell "the rest of the story." We were processing not only for ourselves but also for all the victims of the Inquisition. What we experienced was proof enough that the trauma of catastrophic events such as the Inquisition, the Trail of Tears, the Revolutionary War, the Civil War, the Killing Fields of Cambodia, of all the macabre actions of humankind, hangs heavily in our midst and in our souls, though unseen.

I was enormously grateful when we crossed over into the majestic Pyrenees region of France. The odor of smoke stopped instantly. My happiness quotient soared even though my lungs remained distressed. The travel through the beautiful mountains was uplifting. There was a palpable sense of late fall preparing to yield soon to the austerity of winter. How auspicious to arrive at Lourdes at the end of the seasonal time for shedding.

LOURDES

Lourdes, city of healing hope for untold millions, has an amazing story. On November 2, 1858, Bernadette Soubirous, a sickly fourteen-year-old girl who was unschooled in catechism yet ever most devoted to God, mystically encountered a "beautiful lady." She did not recognize the Lady, yet returned unhesitatingly to the Grotto of Massabielle to experience a total of eighteen apparitions and messages. Lay people who believed in the apparitions gathered to watch as Bernadette conversed with the invisible Lady. The local authorities were skeptical, especially the parish priest. He refused to believe that an uneducated child could be having such encounters until the day Bernadette told him the Lady's name was "The Immaculate Conception." When asked if she understood what this name meant, Bernadette said that she did not. Thus began a change in the priest's attitude.

Subsequently, most onlookers thought Bernadette had lost her mind when she followed Mother Mary's instructions to dig in the earth with her bare hands. Despite their scorn, Bernadette continued digging until she reached water. This water became the source for the healing baths for which Lourdes is famous. People from all faith traditions have traveled ever since from all over the world in search of healing intercession by Our Lady of Lourdes. They come to pray as well as to immerse in the baths. Volumes of medically documented miraculous healings stand as testimony to the sacredness of this site.

Lourdes was the final destination for our group. While the commercialism of the holy site was initially offputting, the actual experience was not. I felt the healing energy begin to work inside me while I meditated on a bench outside the baths. The bath itself was breathtaking—not in beauty, but rather, in temperature. All I could manage while being dunked by the angelic attendants in my white sheet wrap was a meager gasp of pure shock at the coldness of the water. In and out in an instant, I was frozen speechless. All night long into the next day, every cell of my body vibrated, so much so that I did not sleep the entire night. When I returned home to the USA, still sick with near-pneumonia, it seemed as though I had completed everything for which I been born. The slate was clear, void of all script. That chapter of my life was over. It was strange. I did not know what to do.

Up to that point, I had lived my life in relative accordance with the norm. I had raised a family, socialized, played and worked within the approved cultural paradigms. The rebirth in 1985 promoted deeper inner work through years of good psychotherapy followed by three years' immersion in an excellent post-master's clinical program that required deep introspection. Eventually, the experiences I was having no longer fit into the conventionally held psychotherapeutic belief system. According to traditional clinical paradigms, it seemed that I was having a breakdown, because only crazy people have visions, hear voices. and see blue light enveloping them in their beds at night. I knew I was not crazy even though my friends, family, colleagues and psychotherapist wondered. Of necessity, I proceeded to go it alone while continuing to work on myself through spiritually focused retreats and healing practices further enhanced by bodywork of a variety of modalities. Yet I was not alone. I had begun to meet others who also felt compelled to pursue the mysterious clues and paths that were opening up for them.

During 1996, I began to hear an inner voice telling me that it was time to sell the house I really loved. I ignored it. I had one child left at home and no intention of going anywhere. She needed me, and I wanted to enjoy the remainder of her high school experience with her. While entering the driveway on an August, 1997 afternoon, I watched in astonishment as an unseen force shoved my sturdy post mailbox to the ground. Bizarre as it sounds, I knew that it was time to list the house. I called a realtor friend that day. The house sold about a year to the day later, right after I had delivered my daughter to college.

Next, I understood that I was to let go my career, close up shop. I had grown ready to release the house after coming to the realization that I used very little of its total space, what with my children grown and essentially gone. I also no longer had the inclination or the help to maintain it properly. My interests lay elsewhere. However, letting go the primary source of income and a career that I loved was an entirely different matter. I just could not see how that was going to work. Again, I ignored the clear nudge.

One fine day in April 1999, right in the middle of a session, a car hit a corner of my office. The man whose car it was came to the door in a state of shock; he scratched his head and said he had no idea how that could have happened. He had merely been slowly easing his vehicle out of the driveway behind the building. I, though, knew what had happened. It was time to let go of the lease to the office that I loved. Sounds crazy, but it's true. I tend to get very physical messages if I'm not listening to the more subtle ones. The lease renewal documents had been sitting in the "in" basket on my desk. My client was not hurt, just surprised as were the unsuspecting driver and I. No further reminders needed, I let go the office without saying a word and, on a per hour basis, leased space from colleagues. The new arrangements were just not the same. Before the November, 1999 pilgrimage to Fatima and Lourdes, I closed my practice.

The purpose and focus of my life had changed completely. After Lourdes, I even left family, friends, colleagues, and all sense of the familiar to head southwest to live in an informal spiritual community in Arizona. As I drove south along the eastern seaboard before heading west on I-40, the strangest thing happened. At the border where Virginia meets North Carolina I felt a sensation, like a snap, that was accompanied by an image that I, like a dolphin, had escaped through a hole in a tightly woven fishing net. I obviously had broken free of something. My time in Arizona was brief, lasting only from the end of December, 1999 to the day before Cinco de Mayo, May 5, 2000. I actually knew by the end of

February that it was time to leave, but after years of having a home, I was not yet adapted to living the nomadic lifestyle that would continue for ten years. It took another big push to get me to pack up and go. That has now become a predictable pattern: first the message that it is time to leave, followed by some kind of dramatic intervention to get me to actually do it if I don't respond in a timely manner.

The catapult of the pilgrimage to Fatima and Lourdes hurled me from a provincial, somewhat locally lived life to one of world exploration with every aspect of my self ever more focused on God. I have met and studied with interesting, sometimes quite challenging, spiritual teachers from all sorts of traditions. I have visited well-known as well as offbeat regions of my own country and other nations that are treasures of Mother Earth's unbelievable beauty. The national parks of the United States are our holy temples. Other nations have cathedrals and mosques. Having met people from all faiths, races and cultures, I am continually convinced of the essential goodness of the human species despite what the media reports. This is why I seldom watch television or read the news—it's distorted and unconscionably incomplete.

TESTS AND LESSONS

Can you imagine my excitement when given a second shot at life? I left a black and white existence to live life in full Technicolor. Turned on, I was hungry to learn and all atwitter in the vastness of this expanded world-view. I wanted to share with anyone and everyone who would listen. I was open and full of love. I was happier than I had ever been, with two exceptions: giving birth to and then parenting two precious children. The beginning of the spiritual awakening process is a time of great exhilaration. When the lights go on, the lights go on! There is a sense of magic, ease and grace. Insights flow with unparalleled spontaneity. It is a beautifully uplifting time.

At a certain juncture, though, the going gets tougher. The spiritual curriculum includes an ongoing series of initiations and tests. Initially, the beginning student does not even know that such things as spiritual tests exist.

True knowing comes through lived experience. No book in the world can supplant knowledge earned through visceral experience. For each of us, the goal is to master each lesson so that we can proceed on to the next set of lessons. It is like the tests given from grade school all the way through university. Pop quizzes come when you least expect them, no warning given!

Let us turn to the concepts of the Divided Line, the Allegory of the Cave, and the Sun, presented by the ancient Greek philosopher Plato in his book, *The Republic* as translated by Francis MacDonald Cornford. In my opinion, Plato actually describes how the lights go on when our soul makes the leap in consciousness by freeing itself from the bondage of illusion that is the shadowy world of the Cave, the world of ordinary, artificial reality. As our soul travels the Divided Line from shallow, face-value perception to Sun-illumined depth perception, the realm of infinite universal knowledge opens up. Ordinary reality, the everyday world, the world we have been taught is all there is, gives way to an ever-unfolding vaster reality. Through this illumination, our sense perception takes a quantum leap.

Now factor in the Sunlight on Water concept brought to us by The Ones With No Names. In this place of unified consciousness, we are able to anchor heaven on earth. The emanating aspect of God, the seed of love that we are that has dropped down from the Absolute, illumines our body through our soul. This is ascension. This is what Jesus and Mary and all other avatars have been showing us. Enabled through the ascendant leap of faith into the greater consciousness afforded by traveling Plato's Divided Line, we bring the loving light into our selves and back into the world. This is how we heal and grow our soul. This is how we can change the world.

Nonetheless, things can get a little tricky because we have entered into a curriculum that is out of this world, at least out of the "normal" world of ordinary consciousness. Deeper teachings, perceptions, realms, and dimensions become available. There are many ways to access the greater universities of knowledge that become accessible once we take the leap. During the dreamtime, we attend "night school" with master teachers. Night school is spiritual school. Meditation is another vehicle for downloading spiritual teachings. Sitting in silence, spending unhurried time in nature are two more. As we learn, we are tested. The quizzes and the lessons continue until mastery is accomplished. Then the next set of lessons and tests appear. For me, the lessons have been predominantly experiential rather than academic. I call these sets of lessons learning modules.

The curriculum is quite diverse in spectrum as you can see from the range of experiences I have been sharing with you. Here is an example of a distinctly different sort of a module. As you read, remember that everything is learning. Do not judge, please. This course of study has been an essential part of my learning curve that has proven helpful to others who are relieved when they can talk freely about their own experiences.

One day in the early 1990's, a catalogue from Omega Institute arrived in the mail. Omega is a well-established conference facility in upstate New York that offers an interesting, diverse, spiritually oriented curriculum. The catalogue opened to the page that announced an upcoming weekend class with Dr. John Mack, well-known Harvard psychiatrist, on the subject of alien abduction. My reaction was strange, for I had a lifelong interest in extraterrestrial life. However, for some reason I thought, "Well, Omega has just gone over the edge by offering this course. They're going to lose all credibility." I slammed the catalogue shut but did not toss it into the trash.

Within the month that followed six individuals called for help with alien abduction trauma. They did not know each other. Out came the catalogue and I was on the phone to register for Dr. Mack's class in a flash. This was a learning module! Evidently, it was time to understand more about the phenomenon so that I could be of assistance to people with this issue. The class was excellent, just chock full of information and wonderful participants. Two clinicians were present, a psychologist and myself. Everyone else was an abductee. The abductee group included a government secret agent, the CEO of a high tech computer company, a leading journalist, healers, businesspersons, and mothers. This was a well-educated, articulate, accomplished group of individuals. Dr. Mack was credible, well prepared and balanced in his research methodology and work with patients. His compassion for those who have had such unnerving encounters was exemplary.

A courageous man, Dr. Mack endured ferocious backlash for speaking out on the hush-hush subject of extraterrestrial abduction. His book *Abduction, Human Encounters with Aliens*, has reassured thousands of abductees worldwide. The United States military tried to silence him by offering unlimited money and research opportunities as long as he never disclosed the findings. Dr. Mack, a man of integrity, refused. His commitment was to his patients. Multiple closed-door sessions held in an attempt to fire him from his post at Harvard were unsuccessful due to the outpouring of international support for his groundbreaking work. It was with sadness that I learned about his death in 2004 in London by hit-and-run as he crossed the street to attend a conference.

The course turned out to be quite an important piece in the ladder of my learning, including the realization that I, too, had had abduction experiences. I vividly recalled one night when I laid in my bed completely immobilized while someone or something probed my ovaries. This was not a dream state. I was wide awake. I could not open my mouth to scream or move my arms and legs to get whoever was doing this away from my body. I could not see the perpetrators, but I surely did feel the tugging in my body. The next day my pelvis was sore, especially in my ovaries. This abduction experience was qualitatively different from the blue light bedtime visitations by The Ones With No Names. The latter were pleasant, comforting, uplifting. The abduction experience was neither pleasant nor consciously consented to in any way on my part.

Now I had officially entered into what would become an ongoing course of study. Subsequently, I have met many people over the years—government and civilian—who have knowledge about and have experienced such encounters. This is a most complicated subject. Suffice it to say, we are definitely not alone. The good news is that we do have many wonderful friends from other planets and galaxies who are here to support and help us, not hurt us.

The time is now appropriate to tell you about my introduction to Platonic philosophy. Not long after attending Dr. Mack's workshop, I had an unusual encounter with a small black spider while working in my kitchen. It was about three-eighths of an inch in diameter, and, as it watched me from the side of the countertop, it telepathically indicated that it wanted to sit in meditation with me. Truthfully, this made me rather nervous. I agreed to join it in meditation with the condition that it stayed still. It was to stay put while I sat on the floor with my eyes closed. No jumping onto me! Our agreement struck, I went into instant altered state, and to my amazement, was given a symbol. With this short, to-the-point interaction, the meditation ended.

Puzzled as to the symbol's meaning, I asked two friends, both academics, if they knew what it meant. Each, separately, without hesitation, told me that it represented Plato's Divided Line. Never having read Plato, I hustled to get my hands on a copy of *The Republic*, a collection of his discourses. Conceptually, the interpretation of the symbol made sense. Recently a friend questioned me about it, said it did not look like the picture of Plato's Divided Line in the book. I reread the section on the Divided Line, the Allegory of the Cave, and the concept of the Sun. My friend was correct. The symbol that came through in that meditation actually integrated all three concepts into one. What an efficient idea, little black spider!

I have placed this discussion about Platonic philosophy in this section of the book because the interaction occurred during the ET learning module. Paperwork I was filling out at the time for Dr. Mack's Program for Extraordinary Experience Research, PEER, happened to be lying on top of the counter. The black spider crawled into and then out of the accompanying envelope just to punctuate its interstellar connection. One could fairly ask then, who was Plato and where did he come from? I joyfully leave you to quest for that answer!

Some places and beings we just do not need to visit. To be honest, it is a bit of a challenge to tease out what we do need to experience and what we do not. When we are in the thick of the story, objectivity often yields to the moment at hand. However, we do have some choice in the matter. For instance, we do not need to drive the car off a bridge to understand it will sink in the river and we might drown. The pitfalls blatantly clear, we know better than to take such unnecessary risks. Yet we humans do love the grand adventure. Thrilled by the unknown, we will travel to the ends of the earth, and beyond, to explore new frontiers. Sometimes what comes our way is so intriguing, so interesting, and so seductive that we just plunge on in without sensible, thoughtful regard for the consequences. That old saying, "Curiosity nearly killed the cat," is a wise one. Another good analogy would be of the toddler who spies the electric socket and thinks, "Hmmm, I wonder what that is? I think I'll just go stick my pinkie in that hole." Well, you know the rest of that story. We have all lived it and it is simply shocking!

Do you remember those tests? They arrive with a capital "T." First, we awaken. With widened perceptual capacity comes a host of reassuring otherworldly support through our personal spirit guides and angels. After a period of encouragement by our spiritual cheerleaders come tests of discernment to see if we're going to put our fingers into the socket. Are we going to slow down enough to ask, "Hey, what is this? Can I, *should* I put my pinkie in there?"

There really is no judgment about which decision we make. There is no wrong way. There are shorter ways. There are longer ways. There are gentle ways. There are hard ways. However, please do know that there are no shortcuts. I learned that lesson one day while attempting to cut time off a run to do errands in between appointments. Avoiding traffic, I thought I could get to my destination faster by cutting through side streets in the neighborhood. Suffice it to say, the shortcut took twice as long. I went full circle, had to start all over again back at the starting gate. At that moment, the booming voice of White Waters came through. With authority he said, "There are no shortcuts!" This is how spiritual school works. I just thought I was going to the store. The lesson gained from this misadventure has never left me.

I cannot say emphatically enough how important it is to stop, look, and listen. It is okay to step back and take time to make an assessment. We are not in the Indy 500. You know what happens on that fast track — a lot of crashes. It really is okay to proceed with caution. Ask questions until you've gathered enough information to help you decide which way to go. We live in a ridiculously fast-paced world. We're pushed to move, think, eat, run, and spend faster and more. The faster we go, the less aware we are. We take little time to step out of the craziness for contemplative moments. We don't think that we have time to stop, look, and listen. When we do stop, we often get the answers we've been seeking. Time out of the rat race to consider the most prudent course of action is essential.

One of the wisest teachings I ever encountered came from a White Mountain Apache elder. I read it in a little book many years ago, the name of which I've forgotten. In essence, he said, "On the first instinct, don't go. On the second impulse, do not go. On the third, stay still. On the fourth, proceed." Reread that wisdom slowly. Let it be absorbed. The process of letting the dust settle for purposes of making the wisest decision may take an hour, a day, a month, a year, even several years in some instances. This pearl of wisdom from the White Mountain Apache elder can literally and probably already has saved lives.

I, in my unrefined thirst to learn, unsuspectingly fell into a dark force craftily woven trap. This happened faster than I could yell, "Stop!" The person I met that fateful day masterfully shape-shifted before me into a shaman from a rainforest somewhere in South America. Brown-skinned with bowl-cut jet-black hair, he wore, in the traditional way, only a loincloth. That is what I saw with my eyes wide open. He exuded the essence of plant medicine and expert shamanic knowledge. He gave promise of convivial camaraderie. Unbeknownst to me, he had already honed in by psychic spying to find the unmet need areas of my life. He read me well, exposed himself before my eyes once he knew how he would proceed. He knew I had a strong interest in shamanism with a bent towards the South American vintage. My metaphysical interests and experiences had already distanced friends and colleagues, even my analyst. I tended to overwork. I traveled when I could to be with people of like mind. Although I immediately sensed great danger about this person, his adept display hooked me, as he knew it would. I wondered what he knew, what he could teach me about herbs and healing. That was the promise that dangled so enticingly in the air. In that moment of heightened curiosity, I dropped my guard, which allowed him to barge right on in and psychically lock into my heart, mind and soul.

Heed those danger warnings. They happen for good reason. That override of intuition cost me emotionally for years. I had not learned enough to stop, look, and listen to the signal system used by my wonderful team of Divine Self, Guides, and Teachers to give warning. I was ripe for the picking in my metaphysical naïveté. Psychically wide-open, far too trusting, always looking to find the good in others, innately curious, and, untrained in psychic protection, I lacked the knowledge and tools I needed. From a position of secure sacred space, it is possible to detect the true nature of incoming energies. A clean inner and outer environment allows one time to assess whether or not to engage with approaching energies. I did not know enough to take such precautions when that magician put his tentacles into me.

Friends and colleagues had no experience with the kinds of phenomena I would describe to them. Weird manifestations had become frequent in all areas of my life. Even experts in the psychiatric field—and I did make calls for help when I had clients who presented unusual symptoms—were not helpful. I just kept going forward on my own, trying to negotiate my way through the fascinating maze. I had not yet learned to put out a strong call for assistance from the spirit realms. Years later, I found help among medicine people and in esoteric metaphysical teachings. The knowledge I needed and what to do with it was in the unspoken and hidden teachings. Of greatest benefit, however, was and continues to be the development of a solid working relationship with my inner guidance.

This particular story has a strange history. I unknowingly walked right into a trap of revenge that was cultivated over thousands of years. Yes, another past life experience, this one from the time of The Flood. The individual in question died before getting into a safe place. He blamed me for his death. He actually verbally told me that in present time. In that ancient terrible time of decision I had but two choices: close the door to the safe place, in which case hundreds would survive, or wait for him to return from his travels, in which case most likely everyone would perish. It wasn't really a choice. Outside the safe zone, this poor soul experienced suffering beyond comprehension, which he then nurtured over millennia into murderous proportions.

Possessed, he entered lifetime upon lifetime to go after me and anyone else he thought had wronged him—without any moral scruples whatsoever. He had so joined with the dark that he had no compunction about entangling, poisoning, and strangling others and me in his vicious web. At the same time, he had great gifts. He could be hilariously funny. On occasion even the golden energy of an angel would shine through. Others saw and felt this, too. He was unbelievably adept in the metaphysical arts. For instance, he had a bowl of flowers cut two years prior. The flowers should have been dead, dead, dead. However, these vibrant, colorful flowers continued to open each morning all colorful and perky and to close up again at dusk no matter what the season. He could project out of his body during the night and return in the morning with physical objects secured during his travels. He could make a fire soar from mere embers with just a thought.

Yet his Machiavellian ways, operative below the surface, could not remain hidden. The dark simply cannot indefinitely hide itself from the Light. The black magician's façade eventually crumbled. With the excellent assistance of Mother Mary, White Waters, and my mother serving as mission operatives from the "other side," I was able to extricate myself from the situation. Somewhat, as it turned out. He stealthily psychically continued to stalk me until I learned how to cut the energy cords that he had so cleverly imbedded into my chakra system. The cord cuttings were helpful, created a clear zone in which I could usually detect when he was up to his old stalking tricks. Ten years it took to comprehend just how finely woven that trap actually was. I had distorted memory for time, place, conversations, and events that had occurred. The encasing was fog-like, designed to keep me entrapped.

There is a concept in psychiatry called thought insertion. When a patient reports that someone has been putting thoughts into his head, the assumption is usually that he is suffering from delusions. My encounters have taught me that thought insertion does happen. In addition to my own experiences, I have witnessed perpetration attempts against individuals psychically astute enough to know when the black magician was trying to force something into their minds. They knew what he was doing and angrily called him on it. Thought insertion is real. It is psychic assault.

We need only to look at the power of suggestion utilized through hypnosis. Subliminal advertising is another form of thought insertion. Mind control research projects, and there are many, are specifically that, no explanation needed. Adept individuals can project thoughts into those spaces in your mind and body to impact thought, perception, behavior, emotions, even your physical health. That's one way they try to control you. I have heard a number of stories from indigenous teachers on this subject. I have lived through unanticipated ordeals while learning much that has proven to be immensely helpful for others as well as for me. This learning curve has enabled me to regain parts of myself that had been scattered through eons of time. I think the Girl Scout motto, "Be Prepared," is a good one. Knowing about a subject doesn't mean you're inviting such energies in. Learn, detach, and do not give away your power. Not knowing, I believe, is more hazardous to your health.

Recently I was gifted the book *Psychic Discoveries*, which provides an excellent discussion of some of the extrasensory perception research conducted in Russia. The scientific development and application of psychic abilities is the focus. A concern repeatedly expressed by some of the scientists interviewed is the potential for misapplication of such research for purposes of mass, as well as individual, mind control.

Psychic abilities are gifts that are neither good nor bad. How one chooses to apply those gifts, however, is the primary concern. That there is potential for harm as well as potential for good is real.

I highly recommend as well the book by Dr. David Morehouse, *Psychic Warrior: Inside the CIA's Stargate Program, The True Story of a Soldier's Espionage and Awakening*. Dr. Morehouse tells the story of the awakening of his paranormal senses after they were shocked into action by a bullet. The story he tells is an important one about use for good or use for ill of psychic abilities. Since healing from his trauma, he has chosen to teach remote viewing to help others develop and utilize their innate gifts for humanitarian purposes and for their personal spiritual development.

KNOWLEDGE IS POWER

While I wish I had listened to the goose-bumped shivery warnings about the black magician, I certainly learned a lot about the ways of the dark ones through exposure to him and others of similar selfish intent. I still believe there is an essential goodness in all humans. After all, we are the Immaculate Conception. We are the incarnated out-breath of God. All over the world, I have met wonderfully loving people who would give you the last cracker in their cupboard. However, not everyone has others' best interests at heart. Not everyone plays by the same rules or abides by the codes of integrity, fairness, informed consent, and truth. There are individuals and groups of people and beings, seen and unseen, that take delight in penetrating our minds, hearts and spirits with subtle, strategically placed psychic manipulations. Let's not let them.

Some are completely conscious in their machinations. With others, it is a case of the right hand not knowing what the left hand is doing through the subconscious and the unconscious mind. If you confront such individuals about a psychic attack, they will usually say, "I don't know what you're talking about. I didn't do that. I didn't say that. You're crazy." So you cannot confront. It is much better to be aware and prepared. Truth is, there are just some people and energies we don't need to associate with. To walk away is self-loving. Self love along with self care is the critical choice here. Such expressions of what has turned away from the Light exist within us, too. This is why the call to do our inner work has been so strong.

Most of us born and raised in the western world are culturally and spiritually naïve. This is a metaphysical handicap. Those who carry knowledge about such things have been the target of systematic extermination for thousands of years. Yes, an overt policy of massacre of specific groups of people has been part of the drama of the conquest of races, religions, species, and continents. Of course, I am speaking here particularly about the indigenous people of this planet, people of the earth-based traditions, and teachers of vast systems of spiritual and medical knowledge in the Far East. Those who grow up learning "the original teachings" understand such things. They know about this field of play, who to go to for help. and how to handle what comes up. They don't talk about it much, but they do know about it.

During the time of the Inquisition, the dark forces worked their way through the Catholic Church to kill off the wisdom teachers, the herbalists, the wise women ways, and knowledge of the empowered Divine Feminine. The attempt was to eradicate all points of view that diverged from official church doctrine. Those in power sought absolute control over the lives and minds of everyone alive. The Inquisition was a bleed-through from hell. Those slithering negative forces did their utmost to destroy the knowledge that can help us to heal our bodies, minds, and spirit. They sought to extinguish all avenues that would enable us to connect with God independently. Their goal was spiritual and economic enslavement. Without people of ancient knowledge to turn to, the rest of the population would not be able to withstand further attack. The dark thrives through fanning the fires of fear.

I appreciate the work of Father Gabriel Amorth. Former Chief Exorcist for the Vatican, Father Amorth raises a current deep and legitimate concern in his book, *An Exorcist Tells His Story*. He exhorts the Church to recognize how serious this problem of spirit possession and psychic attack truly is. His books provide excellent, honest accounts of his work as an exorcist. He has made substantive, valuable contributions to this body of knowledge.

The Catholic Church has been an undeniable conduit through which the dark has woven its tangled and sticky web. Yet *all* religions and spiritual traditions, when honest, can admit to similar sad sagas. Evidence abounds of ungodly influence in every area of life from government to the military to banking to religion to science to secret societies and mystery schools to shamanism and even through the arts.

I want to state clearly that I also absolutely recognize that much compassionate, loving work is accomplished through the shining light of the Divine that is found in illumined individuals and communities within these institutions.

Looked at from this perspective, we have a lot of catch-up learning to do.

No matter where I travel in the world, people are puzzled. They wonder what is going on. They often cannot define what it is that bothers them, but they definitely know that something is amiss. Grandmother Twylah predicted this about the time in which we now live. Gram was a teacher of ancient philosophy and prophecy. She said, "People aren't going to know what's happening to them." By this, she meant that the impact of the turmoil in the unseen realms upon our thoughts, emotions, and bodies would be great. This is why she emphasized the importance of taking responsibility for our own thoughts, words, and actions, and adhering with discipline to a strong spiritual practice.

Fortunately, not all the teachers and elders have died. Fortunately, not all the original knowledge has sunk into oblivion. If you are experiencing something that feels discordant, stop, look, and listen. Confusion accompanied often by a sinking feeling in the gut can be one of the signals that truth within or without is off somehow, that something else might be at work in the shadows. Go within for guidance in the name of the Christ. Go within in the name of Love. Ask for help from someone who you trust. Keep asking, inside and out, until you gain reasonable understanding. You have the God-given right to insist upon the absolute truth.

Understand that there are Masters of Light, masters of dark, and shadow masters. The latter are those who play both sides in these final years of the age of duality called the Fourth World. Stay away from them. They are artful seducers. Some will promise to teach "the" way to enlightenment. Some will say that they have "the" ticket to heaven. No one, no sole group has *the* way. Run from anyone and any organization that says that. They will take your money, your time, your life force energy, and possibly your soul. They will suck you dry. Become astute in your capacity to discern who is standing in Truth and who is not.

This particular learning module is one that each of us will eventually encounter on our spiritual path. Do not be afraid. Be strong! Stand in your power! Be adamant in your resolve. Use this short, powerful, empowering declaration:

> I am the light!
> I am the light of the universe!
> I am the light and
> the light I will remain!

Command this mantra three times in succession with authority as needed. Make a clear statement to the universe that you have made your choice. Make this choice over and again. Non-love energies squirm, often vacate, in the presence of such positive affirmation.

I have chosen to look at such encounters described above as opportunities to re-dedicate myself to God, to be more loving, to do and be the best that I can and to stand in truth and integrity. My mother loved the Golden Rule: "Do unto others as you would have them do unto you." She said this so often when I was growing up it was annoying. Nevertheless, the advice is excellent. See such occasions as tests of your level of commitment to love and to serve others. Do you stand firmly for love? Do you refuse to allow yourself to be distracted from what you really know to be truth? We are the beloved, cherished, radiant children of God. Just say thank you to the dark for these opportunities for refinement and move on up the road.

The unfinished business with the black magician from untold numbers of lifetimes needed to come to the surface for proper resolution. I have forgiven him. I do not like how he operates, but I do understand how he came to be the way he is. I could not help him. Three times, I took him to meet gifted medicine people. Each time, the focus turned on me with this question: "Which way do *you* choose? You have to decide." The lesson was mine. I could not continue to associate with him if I was going to seek soul redemption. Initially deeply ashamed, I have forgiven myself for falling into that well-constructed trap due to my unbridled, naive curiosity. Subsequently, I have been able to help others who have found themselves in similar predicaments. While the attainment of knowledge about dark forces and power-driven black arts magicians was not on my consciously chosen list of things to do, the learning earned has been worthwhile.

THE DEVIL INCARNATE

There is one more story of a related nature that requires telling. This particular story began to surface during my Soul Recognition with Flo Aeveia Magdalena back in 1994. While watching the beautiful shining lights bouncing on the ceiling and hearing celestial music, I heard the name Mephistopheles. Though vaguely familiar, I did not know whom he was or what he had to do with me. After the retreat ended, I looked him up. I was shocked to learn that Mephistopheles is another name for Satan. Why I heard this name remained a big question mark, a mystery unsolved, until 2006.

The details of the story came during a trip to John of God and the Casa de Dom Inacio in Brazil. While there, I received several emails from colleagues encouraging me to attend a fall event in New York City with their spiritual teacher. For years, every time anyone ever asked me to come meet him, I would decline with knots in my belly. Quite unfathomably irritated this time, I decided to submit a prayer request to gain understanding about my inexplicable almost ballistic response to seeing or hearing the teacher's name. While writing the request, what spontaneously poured out of my hand through the pen and onto the paper was an angry exclamation to God. I silently wrote-yelled with all my might, exclaiming, "How could you possibly allow him onto this planet in this time!" I began to see, as though I was watching a movie, how I had literally relinquished my soul in an attempt to save his eons ago during a similar time of great battle between dark and Light. Loving this man, I gave over my soul in a misguided attempt to save him from falling deeper and deeper into the dark. The Mephistopheles riddle was solved. Ever since that fateful yielding, I had been working, lifetime after lifetime, to redeem that part of my soul. Now I understood my periodic concern that I would not make it all the way home, meaning not make it back into the Light by the end of this lifetime. I also understood the source of the previously inexplicable anger.

It seemed that to bring resolution to this unpleasant business, I needed to attend his event in New York City. I was not happy about having to pay for this. However, wanting to be done with it, I went with a definite chip on my shoulder. I wondered if there would be any recognition and apology by him. While I found him a bit cocky in demeanor, the teacher displayed extraordinary healing gifts. He was engaging, charismatic, and delightfully hilarious. About one third of the way into the morning, in the presence of probably just less than five hundred people, the teacher asked if there was someone in the audience by my first name. He struggled with the syllables of my last name. My colleagues filled in the blanks and gave him the rest of my name. He asked me to stand up. As I did, he publicly acknowledged the truth of our historical relationship, apologized, and said, "I've come a long way since then. Back then I was the devil incarnate."

The chip on my shoulder dissolved. I do not know what more I could have asked for. I received absolution through validation, with witnesses to boot! What an amazing gift. His acknowledgement concluded a most important soul retrieval that had begun in 1994. I felt a profound sense of deep inner peace akin to what I experienced that night on the front steps with my mother. I want to be clear here that I also recognized that the anger I had been carrying was mine. Also, while I thought him to be cocky, so was I. What happened to me was not his fault. I made an erroneous choice way back when, thinking I could do something to save him, but that really was not a choice for me to make. He had to choose whether he would stand with God or not. The ancient anger dissolved on the spot to set me free. The teacher and I spoke again privately at the end of the weekend. He gave me a beautiful white rose. Then we parted on excellent and the most respectful and loving of terms.

Blessings upon blessings cascaded upon me after leaving the workshop. Even the cabbie that drove me to the train station soared into a state of bliss! Grumpy and taciturn when I got into his taxi, his demeanor shifted so dramatically that I had to ask what was happening to him. The cabbie said, dreamily, "I just can't talk right now. I'm somewhere else and it's so beautiful!" We giggled. Love energy set loose from this soul reunion and clearing continued to spread out in all directions as I walked with the white rose the teacher had given me to the train station located in the Twin Towers site in New York City. It was the anniversary date of the 9/11/2001 catastrophe. Because the President of the United States was in town, police officers lined the entire corridor around the site. Several female officers commented on the beauty of the white rose and asked where I had been to receive such a flower. I just told them that I had spent the day in the fullness of God's love. That seemed explanation enough for all of us.

What a big learning this particular timeline event has been. No matter what, do not ever give up your soul to save someone else. Yes, we are here to help one another. However, we must take care of ourselves first if we are to be of service to anyone else. This is not being selfish. This is self-love, not narcissism. The events taking place now go far beyond what meets the eye. They are much more than physical. The battle is for our souls. We are the blue ribbon prizes. Rule #1 in wilderness rescue training: do not put your own life at risk. Step back, assess the situation, and proceed accordingly. If we become "lost souls" by mistakenly giving up our souls or any portion thereof, we are not helping anyone and least of all ourselves. Remember what White Waters said: "We are here to heal our souls." The good news—and this *is* good news—is that both the "devil incarnate" and I, with my own obvious share of darkness (cockiness, anger, projection, reluctance to forgive, to name some of the manifestations), show that the process of redemption is possible, that we can find our way back out of the abyss.

Do not succumb to the seductions of those who would entice you into making such an unfortunate choice. They are tricksters. I mistakenly carried forward deep anger at the "devil incarnate." While some of the anger was frustration born through lifetimes of trying to get free only to sink back down into the miasma, some of it I definitely misplaced onto him rather than take responsibility for the unfortunate decision I made so long ago. Sometimes the choices we have to make are heart-wrenching tough ones. Krishna counseled Arjuna that he had to make this same decision during the Kurukshetra War, the epic battle of Indian antiquity documented in the *Bhagavad Gita*. Arjuna had to choose between saving himself by taking a stand against the evil that attacked through the form of beloved family members or by falling along with them by not taking a stand. He did not want to hurt them. He could not have it both ways. He had to choose. He took his stand against evil (non-love).

I decided to share this quite personal story with you because we are living in times that place us at similar risk. Energies have reappeared that would like nothing more than to take our very souls. They are experts at their job. Masters of disguise, charming, handsome and beautiful, classy, they have all the right moves. They speak the words we like to hear. Smooth operators, some even blithely cite scripture and the names of God to entice. They tell us everything we want to hear, which is not necessarily what we *need* to hear. They make the most wonderful promises. Observe to see if their actions match their words. Are they truly emanating love or is something else at work? This is why it is important to stop, look, listen, and not go until the fourth impulse. Sometimes you must step out of the energy to get a clearer picture. Discernment is so important.

My soul, awakened through the reliving of my birth in 1985, joyfully soared during Vision Quest in 1990 and was set free through Soul Recognition in 1994. While merrily rolling along in this renewed sense of self, the black magician reappeared in my life with the specific goal to take me back down into the bowels of hell. Just like those shows on TV, it was the Ultimate Challenge. Please understand that the dark does not happily release its prey.

For those of you who find yourselves in similar predicaments, I can assure you that you have an abundance of healing assistance from your Divine Self, guides, and angels. This help, along with your grit and unrelenting commitment, makes for perfect teamwork. You must be willing to look yourself square in the eye. You must be willing to be bluntly honest with yourself. While our historical warts and pimples are not exactly lovely, the "Not me!" syndrome really gets in the way. How can we insist upon truth if we aren't truthful with ourselves? Fact is, we all have stuff. Not all of it is pretty. Some of it is downright ugly. So what? Our true selves are exquisite, radiant, dancing beams of sunlight on water. Now is the time to do this deep clearing. The loving assistance available for each of us increases daily. Showing up and having the courage to move through "the stuff" starts the process. All flows naturally once we make this commitment. If we remember that what is without is within, we will realize that we are no different from anyone else. What we see around us and in others is what is in need of tender loving care within us. To believe otherwise is to perpetuate the storyline of the dualistic Fourth World.

The stories so far presented are bizarre yet true. One or more witnesses have been present to validate much of what has occurred. I have not gone in search of the stories. They have risen up as scheduled on the timeline of a supra-ordinate calendar in accordance with my willingness to proceed with the redemption of my soul. If you want a good relevant read, I recommend Deepak Chopra's book, *The Return of Merlin*. Dr. Chopra does a great job in clearly depicting how stories with plots and subplots from different timelines run just below the surface of our everyday lives. Brunonia Barry's riveting *The Map of True Places* provides another excellent framework for understanding how sagas from previous lives play out in the present. While both are works of fiction, the spiritual understandings presented are accurate in my estimation. If you believe in reincarnation, then you understand that each of us has such stories running below the surface. Graduation from the karmic wheel is contingent upon corrective completion of these unfinished storylines.

Despite the synchronicities and validation, I have suffered through periods of doubt. Typical and recurring questions are: Am I headed in the right direction? Am I making the most beneficial decisions? Am I making this all up? How am I going to support myself? Two things generally happen when I allow doubt to creep in. First, everything just stops—all work, all everything abruptly and definitively stops. Second, guidance from my spiritual support system seems to disappear. Typically, the frustration builds until I rant and rave about perceived injustices. Sometimes I privately collapse in a teary heap, feeling quite bereft and God-forsaken. These times of doubt spring from a lack of trust. Usually I have sunk into a deep state of worry about meeting the requirements of physical existence. Having unwittingly disengaged myself from the all-sustaining Source, the "stop" mechanism forces me to go within once more. There is really nowhere else to go in such moments. Once I reconnect, my mood, attitude, and thinking processes begin to shift in a more productive direction. Despair yields to renewed faith, trust, and an all-abiding sense of love and well-being. A plan begins to unfold—usually within moments after letting go of "my" plan to allow "The" plan to unfurl. In addition, my guides reappear. Not that they were ever gone. It was just that during my emotional turmoil, I was unreceptive to their presence.

For instance, from 2002 to 2003 I lived for six months in Colorado. Home at last, I thought, as I moved into this beautiful area full of friends, mountains, and everything necessary for a healthy lifestyle. It was wonderful. I made friends with the prairie dogs who hung out on their rounded mounded stoops during my daily walks. Quickly I developed work and a client base. At the end of three months, the work dissolved. Panicked, I headed to the employment agency. The interview turned into a metaphysical teaching time for agency staff. We had a fun few hours together. However, I left the office without any prospect of finding work. I was over qualified in some areas and terribly under qualified in others, especially computer program expertise.

Simultaneously, I pursued ads in the paper and set up interviews with unsuccessful outcomes. Beside myself, I just did not know what to do. Next, the voicemail system on my home phone stopped working. I could not receive incoming messages. This is not a good thing if you are waiting for that all-important "You're hired" call. Using my cell phone, I reported the problem to the phone company. They checked the lines, said there was nothing wrong. Having already had a rant and rave episode complete with a lusty down-on-my-knees crying jag, I didn't have a clue what to do next. It occurred to me that it might be a good idea to meditate to calm down. Almost immediately, the voices of my Divine Self and guides rang through loud and clear. All caught up in a worry frenzy, I had neglected to go within for a good question and answer session. My team said that everything had stopped because I was not listening. It wasn't that I had become irrevocably unemployable; rather, it was time to move from Colorado. Next, they gave me the date of departure. I was to be on the road to New Mexico no later than ten a.m. on the designated Saturday. I was to leave not one moment later. Not surprisingly, the glitch with the house phone resolved immediately once I sat down for that informative meditation.

I locked myself into the announced schedule by arranging to meet friends at ten a.m. at a café in Denver for a farewell cup of coffee. For the first time ever, the drive from Colorado to New Mexico flowed like water. As I entered the door to the home of friends, a documentary filmmaker was preparing to leave. We spoke briefly. When she found out that I had a history of extraterrestrial encounters, she asked if I would agree to an interview. We set a date for the following week. This is a fine example of the behind-the-scenes orchestration of our lives; that interview was why I needed to leave Colorado by the specified time. Had I arrived even ten minutes later, I would have missed the film producer. The interview was a good time. To my knowledge, the documentary remains incomplete due to an unforeseen shortage of funds for production.

Stoppage in my life has repeatedly made me look at my attitude, thoughts, and behaviors. It is a predictable signal that I have strayed off course somehow. It tells me there is something to which I am not paying attention. Doubt, which is lack of trust and faith, springs to life with a fury when I allow myself to go off course from God. Something has to grab my attention. Remember, too, that some of the stoppage and blockage actually can come from interference by others through different manipulations. Sometimes it happens because the timing is not quite right. Some of the blockages come from unfinished soul work. We usually do not go from A to Z. We proceed from A to B to C and so on. There is a logical order to what happens, even if we do not understand it. It just takes time to get these things figured out.

Sometimes during times of doubt, I receive encouragement through the delivery of laser-precise, timely, to-the-point messages. The delivery is often through someone I do not know. How do I know these messages are for me? I just know through years of experience. You know it when it happens. There is a surreal quality to the interaction. Words are used that have specific relevance to me. Western psychiatry could have a hey-day over this one. It's time for another psychiatric term: ideas of reference. This is when the delusional patient believes that someone or something no one else is witness to is directing whatever is being said or inferred specifically at him. The messages could come through the television, a book, through a stranger, or a family member. As though someone has taken a highlighter like one you'd use in a book, the accentuated message stands out like a neon sign.

As clinicians, we walk a fine line when assessing the sanity or lack thereof of persons who report such events. I have found that line to be even finer since my exposure to the goings on in other dimensions and realms of existence that interface with the world in which we live. If you factor in mind control transmissions, the picture really gets complicated. This is why it is important to have a good, solid working relationship with your Divine Self and guides. They're here to help you with your spiritual evolution. They do not push you to do harmful things to others or to your self. They do not try to manipulate you.

Life is so different when you've crossed that Divided Line. We humans hold precious and with great fierceness our working concept of reality. We do not want to believe that unseen beings from this and other worlds are interacting with us. It can be scary when we first realize that we're not alone, that we are equivalent to dust mites in the Milky Way of creation. We feel exposed and vulnerable. Our world construct, one that provides some sense of security, is shattered. We feel quite small in the big scheme of things. Understandably, we derive comfort from the apparent solidity of our long-standing beliefs. Yet people are sharing similar stories everywhere I travel. This can only mean that either there is a mass psychosis operative, or that there is more to our world than meets the eye.

Years ago, I camped for two days at a remote, beautiful national park in the White Mountain Apache territory of New Mexico. The second morning, while breaking camp, a stranger walked up to me and said, "Not all wanderers are lost." Then she walked away. Since I had apparently signed up for the extended travel plan, woman on the road with a lot of bags, I had been wondering for the umpteenth time if the seemingly rambling route of my journey held any true benefit and purpose. Although I was feeling lost, I apparently was not. This quote from the *Lord of the Rings* delivered by the unknown woman was perfect medicine to quell my sense of discomfort. All I could do was giggle.

Two more messages came on separate days while visiting the Cahokia Mounds, an ancient mound site just across the river from St. Louis. The first had to do with my hair. A woman I had traveled with prior to Cahokia told me I would never get a man unless I dyed my graying hair—upsetting, unsolicited advice. I had no intention to change the color of my hair. As I entered into the Mound complex, a trim middle-aged man with a jaunty bounce to his step approached and said, "Don't do anything to your hair. It's beautiful!" That message was perfect. I felt better instantly. The next day, when leaving the complex, I crossed paths with a woman and a man. The woman looked me straight in the eyes and exclaimed, "Oh, you made it here!" Message delivered, she kept on walking. The effect was like having a gold star placed next to Cahokia Mounds on the list of "must visit" places in my spiritual travel itinerary.

Okay, one more story. A few years ago I was in the northeast traveling south on I-95. After a quick dinner at a restaurant, I hurried to get back onto the highway. However, I could not seem to drive my car anywhere but through the drive-through line of Dunkin Donuts, which I found quite strange. I had been to the same restaurant many times and never had a problem getting back onto the highway. Since no exit appeared available, I proceeded through the drive-through and ordered coffee to go. The beautiful Indian woman who took my order looked at me knowingly through her deep sparkling eyes and said, "You have traveled a very long way. Where have you come from?" Emphatically I said, "Yes, I have." I did not answer the second question. I knew she already knew the answer by her smile. Through her came a progress report that made my heart soar.

These kinds of things actually happen to each of us every day. I absolutely know you receive the encouragement and direction you need on a daily basis. Our helpers consistently come through at just the right moment. Honestly, since Lourdes, I cannot even say this is "my" life anymore. I have realized that "i' is not running the show. The big "I" is navigating. This belief is in no way an abnegation of self-responsibility.

It is simply the recognition that there is more to "me" than I once believed.

One of my favorite books from childhood is *The Little Me and the Great Me*, written by Lou Austin, owner of Capon Springs, the resort my family enjoyed visiting in the mountains of West Virginia and the resort of my Moses experience. Mr. Austin's book tells in story form the same idea that we have a "me" and a "Me." The "me" is ego-driven. "Me" is the transcendent aspect of self. This book, along with another one, *The Littlest Angel* by Charles Tazewell, made lasting impressions on me as a child. The latter boosted my spirits when I did not think that I was good enough for God. As I revisited these books as a parent and read them to my children, I was amazed at the depth of spiritual teaching they contain.

Having doubts does not necessarily have to be a negative thing. Prompts to more thoroughly investigate the circumstances of our life, the decisions we make, the people we meet, the paths we take have good purpose. We must use discernment.

Simultaneous with my departure from Colorado in 2003 was my departure from two spiritual groups with which I had been intimately involved since 2000. Freed, I resumed once again a life of constant travel. During March, 2005, I came into direct contact with the healing energies of medium Joao de Texeira of Abadania, Brazil. While watching a television documentary about the healing work at the Casa de Dom Inacio, I felt energy moving in my body. By the end of the program, it was evident that I had received some welcome healing for a recurrent back problem. This distance healing was the kickoff for much deeper healing of the sciatica that caused pain and numbness in my right leg and foot. By August, I was on my way to the Casa.

I will never forget that first day. As I approached Medium Joao, I had the most holy in-the-physical, eyes wide-open visionary experience since the events of my first Vision Quest. I sensed that I was approaching the Throne of God. I saw two enormous golden Archangels hovering to the left of the throne and an extraordinarily beautiful, larger-than-life woman to the right. The throne radiated brilliant, indescribable light. The woman appeared luminous. She had the enormous eyes that one sees in the Archangels and Masters of Light. She wore a full-length deep blue gown ornately decorated with silver thread, beads and sequins. Her thick dark hair cascaded down her back under the glittering twelve-pointed crown that rested upon her head. Her feet did not touch the floor. She appeared to be about sixteen feet tall. Awed by her beauty, I did not recognize her.

Medium Joao directed me to sit in his room for the duration of the session. Once seated, a voice told me that the beautiful woman's name was Stella Maris. Still in the dark as to who was this beautiful being, I hurried to a computer after the morning session to do a search. I learned that Stella Maris is another name for Mother Mary that means Star of the Sea. During the same session, a voice advised me to go to Fall River, a place unknown to me. I called my sister as soon as I landed back in the United States, asked her if she knew where Fall River is. My sister laughed, said it was in Massachusetts. Following Stella Maris' direction to go to Fall River began a series of events I could never have imagined.

PART THREE
STELLA MARIS LEADS THE WAY

With great expectation, I soon traveled north to Fall River, Massachusetts. The view from the interstate was shocking. The city looked like an industrial graveyard. Skeletons of about a hundred abandoned textile mills dominate the skyline, testimony to what happens when business goes literally goes south, which was indeed what happened to the city of Fall River, once the Cotton Capital of the United States. Seeking cheaper venues, the industrialists moved their textile mills to the deep South. They left behind a large city that continues to this day to reconstruct itself from devastating economic ruin. Nothing is pretty about the forsaken massive brick structures that stare down onto a city that has covered the living, breathing earth with concrete. Fall River felt like a city of death. I did not understand why Stella Maris sent me there. Stunned by this specter, I turned the car around as fast as I could and sped south. Soon, though, I would understand.

Pieces of the puzzle about Fall River came together during my second, third, and fourth visits. On the second visit I went directly to the Chamber of Commerce, always a good place to go when you want to understand what drives a region. The staff member I initially spoke with was wonderful: open, friendly, and puzzled by my appearance. "Why would you want to come here?" he asked. I didn't want to tell him that Stella Maris had sent me. I thought he'd most likely usher me right out of his office, think I was some kind of a nut. Nevertheless, I wasn't going to be let off the hook of his curiosity. He persisted in wanting to know why I was interested in Fall River. Succumbing to his determined pressure, because I realized that Mary was pushing him to ask, I told him about my experience with Stella Maris at the Casa de Dom Inacio. This wonderful man knew about the work of the Casa. Dedicated to Mother Mary like myself, he insisted that I meet a colleague of his who also worked for the Chamber. Further, he was certain that I needed to meet two members of the local clergy. One was the head of a booming Protestant church; the other was a priest. First, I met his colleague. After recounting my Mary story he provided phone numbers for the two clergy while reiterating that yes, yes, yes, I absolutely needed to meet with them.

Later that day I called to arrange an appointment with the Protestant minister, but I did not dial up the priest. I was hesitant. Who was I to talk with a priest about Mary? Would he believe me? Would he discount me, a non-Catholic? A few days later my sister said that the priest had left a message; he wondered if I was coming up for our appointment in view of the inclement weather. I told her that it must have been the Protestant minister because I had not yet called the priest. She insisted the message was from the priest. Okay, okay, I can take a hint! This was one of "those" messages, sent through my sister. I made the call to set up the appointment. Clearly, it was important for me to connect with him.

We met during my third visit to Fall River. This priest was beatific. He radiated a golden light that seemed to grow in magnitude as we talked. For two hours we freely swapped stories of a metaphysical nature. I learned his story, how he came to know Mary and Jesus in a transcendent way through his visits to the pilgrimage site of Medjugorje, Bosnia. Before Medjugorje he had thought apparitions of Mary to be a thing of the past. His first trip to the holy site proved otherwise. During his reluctant initial pilgrimage, he had a profound encounter with the Divine that occurred quite spontaneously—in spite of himself. Knowing about the Holy Spirit through academia is one thing. Receiving the energy of the Holy Spirit is another. The latter is a felt, physical experience. Priest and counselor to priests, his role expanded post-Medjugorje to include the offering of a healing prayer ministry that served many members of the community.

Then the priest began to ask questions of me. Had I traveled to Medjugorje? I said no, that this was the first time I had heard about that holy place. Was I Catholic? No. Married? No, divorced. Silence. After I told him about my Mary experience, he suggested we pray on how to proceed and suggested that I get in touch again in one month. This seemed to be a reasonable idea. However, he was unresponsive to my phone and email messages at the end of the month. We have not communicated since. Perhaps the one meeting was all that was required. I must say I thoroughly enjoyed meeting the lit-up-with-God priest so highly regarded in his community.

Next, I met with the Protestant minister, a delightful, dynamic pastor of keen intellect and devoted public service. We covered a wide range of religiously focused topics during the two hours we spent together. As was the case with the priest, the exchange was open, deep, and intense. We did not waste any time getting into serious discussion. From the minister I learned the "something more" about Fall River. Well known for its economic plight, Fall River unfortunately made the headlines worldwide as the city where disclosures about sexual abuse by priests first surfaced. The disclosures tore open the heretofore heavily guarded secret of the global Catholic Church. The Catholic Diocese of Fall River was devastated. Many parishes closed as parishioners left the Church in great numbers. Some parishioners who left their Fall River parishes in search of a safe place to pray reached out to this particularly beloved clergyman.

Only just short time ago did I fully piece together something else that was revealed to me in 2005. Having moved to Rhode Island, it was necessary to obtain a new driver's license, registration, and tags for my car. After installing the new license plates, the owner of the inspection garage casually asked if I knew to whom the license plate numbers belonged prior to me. Of course I did not know. He then said that Don Bosco was the previous owner. I was surprised and delighted. Don Bosco, known as Saint John Bosco, was an Italian priest who lived during the 1800's. All I knew about him was that he had reported a prophetic dream of a modern city that would be built somewhere in South America. That city is Brasilia, now the capital of Brazil. Begun in 1956, this incredible building project was completed in 1960. President Juscelino Kubitschek's goal was to fulfill the recommendation, written in 1891 in that country's constitution, to move the capital from coastal Rio de Janeiro to a more central, interior location. A favorite spot for visitors to Brasilia is the Cathedral de Dom Bosco, constructed in honor of this visionary saint.[5]

Something tugged at me about Don Bosco. I finally put that dangling participle of information, delivered through the garage owner, into a full sentence. Had he had reincarnated into Rhode Island and driven a vehicle? Was the name a trigger to spur me to investigate the life of this saint? Off to the computer I went. The critical missing piece dropped into place with a blast. Don Bosco's contributions were many. Having grown up in poverty himself, his vocation was to help disadvantaged boys through his "Preventive System of Education," the components of which were love, gentleness, and religion. Education, he said, was a "matter of the heart." Founder of the Salesian order, builder of churches, visionary, Don Bosco revealed a specific fear shortly before his passing:

"I will reveal to you now a fear…I fear that one of ours may come to misinterpret the affection that Don Bosco had for the young, and from the way that I received their confession—really, really close—and may let himself get carried away with too much sensuality towards them, and then pretend to justify himself by saying that Don Bosco did the same, be it when he spoke to them in secret, be it when he received their confession. I know that one can be conquered by way of the heart, and I fear dangers, and spiritual harm."[6]

His precognition has proved completely accurate in view of what has transpired since the first disclosures of sexual abuse by priests were made public in May, 1992. The fallout continues; in fact, has expanded with such serious momentum that the church can no longer deny. The impact, worldwide, strikes at the heart and structure of the Catholic religion.

Having had the opportunity to spend focused quality time with two clerics of substance, I wondered whatever was to come next. What did Mary want of me? I didn't have to wait long for an answer. While working at the computer one afternoon I noticed that a site named Medjugorje Web had somehow found its way into my Favorites section. I didn't put it there, had never heard of the site before. Being the curious woman I am, I clicked the link and began to read about Medjugorje. Next, I called the number provided on the site for details about their group tours. After hanging up from an informative call with the tour leader, I told Mary that though her intent was for me to travel to Medjugorje, I couldn't go right then. I did not have the money. A couple of months went by. Then one day, while I was researching something completely unrelated on the web for a friend, the same Medjugorje website popped up boldly into the Keyword section. I hit the link, read the site once more and said to Mary, "Okay, you don't have to tell me a third time. I'll go." I called a trusty traveling companion, told her it was time for us to go to Bosnia.

As a non-Catholic, this was the most Catholic outing I have ever taken. I practiced Hail Mary's and Our Fathers, Glory Be's and a Jesus Rosary particular to Medjugorje for weeks in advance of our trip. We flew first to Frankfort, Germany, then to Split, Croatia. At Split we were met by a lovely tour guide who discussed the history of the region while we traveled by bus to Medjugorje, Bosnia. The bus traversed a winding mountainous road that overlooked sharp cliffs that plunged down into the crystal blue waters of the Aegean Sea. The beauty of the countryside belied the region's history, as it has been a battleground for unspeakable inhuman massacre and war.

The story of Medjugorje is compelling. The apparitions of Mary began on June 25, 1981. She first appeared on a rugged hill composed of the most jagged, inhospitable rock imaginable. Thereafter, each day at five-forty p.m., she continued to appear to six children: Marija, Mirjana, Vicka, Ivanka, Ivan, and Jakov. Within the first week, word of the apparitions spread like wildfire. Thousands of the faithful and the curious began to flock to the tiny hamlet, home to sheepherders, tobacco growers, and vineyards. The people of Medjugorje opened their hearts and homes to the pilgrims. They shared the little food and water they had without hesitation.

The upsurge of activity in this off-the-road community did not escape the attention of the authorities. At the time when the apparitions began to occur, Bosnia was still part of Yugoslavia, and that nation was

Communist and anti-God. The visionaries and their families survived many challenging trials as the government attempted to poke holes in their stories. The children stood firmly in their convictions. They remained dedicated to the Holy Mother, to Jesus, and to the Catholic Church. Abducted by the authorities and taken to distant medical and psychiatric facilities for evaluation and interrogation, they were under constant surveillance, even bullied at gunpoint. Neighbors became spies, turned against them and their families. Sentinels, posted along the path, tried to block the children from attending their daily meeting with Mary. The strategy was to divide and conquer so that each child would recant. Not one did. As adults, the visionaries continue to stand unified in the experiences that they have shared.

The appearances by Mary presaged by ten years the terrible genocide that began in 1991 among the ethnic and religious peoples of Yugoslavia: the Serbians, the Bosnians, the Croatians. Prior to the genocide, these ethnic groups had lived relatively peacefully side by side. The war ended in 1996. Mary's message through Medjugorje before, during, and since has consistently been that we can stop the wars through prayers and fasting. This certainly proved true for the community of Medjugorje. Battle raged all around but did not enter the city limits. Even fighter pilots who attempted to enter the area had to turn back because of strange fog and mysterious glitches with their instrument gauges. Citizens who lived outside of Medjugorje were the target of unspeakable atrocities during the genocide. Psyches and spirits were shattered. The devastation was incomprehensible. The healing work continues to this day.

Since 1981, millions of people have traveled to Medjugorje from all areas of the globe to pray and to ask for healing. Reports of miraculous intercessions abound. All over the world, people connect to Medjugorje through prayer groups. They eagerly await the monthly messages that Mary sends through one of the visionaries. Our Lady speaks of Her plan, of how the prayers and the fasting support her work on behalf of humanity. Medjugorje is home to some quite impressive model treatment communities to help people who are struggling with drug and alcohol addictions. The cornerstone of these programs is love, devotion, and hard work. These are not time-limited lock-down units. Residents can voluntarily live there for the rest of their lives if they so choose. Drug addiction has been an ongoing terrible plague for people of the region during and ever since the genocide. A drug-addicted, hence morally compromised, military was apparently part of the strategy for the commission of the genocide.

Particularly poignant was our excursion to Uzari, home to the Siroki Brijeg Cathedral and Father Jozo. Father Jozo was the Franciscan priest-in-residence when the apparitions began at Medjugorje. Imprisoned for three years for not recanting his belief that something miraculous was happening through the children, Father Jozo was tortured and starved. His back was broken, his teeth knocked out. Yet he left prison even more passionately devoted. The cathedral where he now serves is famous for another tragic reason. It is the site of massacre of thirty Franciscan priests by the Yugoslavian military on February 7, 1945. Inside the main sanctuary a side chapel stands as memorial to the priests who were shot and burned because they refused to renounce their vows to God. The Yugoslavian military also slaughtered hundreds of thousands of citizens as they returned to their homeland at the end of World War II.

At the beginning of our pilgrimage, we listened to a talk given by Father Svet, a humble, gentle, loving, deeply reflective Franciscan monk. He asked important questions as he talked about the concepts of martyrdom, monuments, and crucifixion. "Why do we remember martyrs?" he asked. He said not to take their lives lightly because their lives are full of meaning and purpose. He said we must be careful what monuments we build. What is their purpose—to show that we are better than others? To show that we are good and others are bad? What kinds of monuments do we build in our heads? Do those monuments improve the quality of our lives? We need to watch out because we tend to repeat mistakes. Are we going to love more, serve the Lord more, or, allow some other forces to lead? Every generation, every nation, every person has its own sin. We have things to remember so that we can correct them. Memories, said Father Svet, are for our own purification of our heart. What do our memories do to us? Do they teach us? Do they cause us to be angry? Do they lead us to revenge? Or do they lead us to redemption and blessings?

He said, "Crucifixion is more dramatic, radical, imposing, and aggressive today than at any other time in history. The deception is so great that the way we behave has become normal. The deception has penetrated the very culture of which we are a part." We are all crucified. We all become crucifiers. He asked, "How do we build a gentle, peaceful culture that would be of God? We do not have to do something extra special. Can we just be gentle with each other? Can we radiate spiritual love? Can we harmoniously fit into the process of Nature that God has created?"

These are important questions. I think often about Father Svet's talk, about the concepts of monuments and crucifixion that he made relevant to the world in which we live.

Medjugorje offers, through its example of dedicated devotional practice, some keys to establishing and sustaining spiritual community in a world gone mad. Practices of prayer and fasting exist in all the world's spiritual and religious traditions, not just in Catholic Medjugorje. Mary encourages us to place God in the center of our homes and families. No matter what path we take to the ultimate Source, establishing a firm pillar of love in the center of our homes and through daily devotional practice makes good sense. Such commitment creates a stability that helps us to stand rooted and strong in the eye of the storms that we are now encountering. Mary's message is not different from other traditions when she says that we have lost our way. Each spiritual and religious tradition has emerged from teachings shared by a master teacher. Each tradition encourages us to embrace the original teachings and to follow the example set by those master teachers. Peaceful, harmonious, respectful co-existence is possible if we get back to basics. When we open to the gifts that are contained in the original teachings and put those pieces together, we have a complete system that brings mind, body, and spirit into balance.

Striking was the diversity of people who came from all around the world to pray in St. James Church each day. With heads bowed in prayer, nuns, priests, Catholics and non-Catholics sat side by side in ecstatic prayer. Pilgrims and clergy return post-pilgrimage to their homes and communities full of Mary's energy and her message of love. I deduced that part of what she wanted me to understand about Fall River is how she is pouring Mother Love into the heart and soul of that distressed city and state. Many pilgrims travel from Massachusetts to Medjugorge.

Mary's present mission continues to be a prophetic one. She has indicated that there will be a series of lead in events prior to a dramatic physical spectacle on the mountain overlooking Medjugorje. When the mountain event happens, she will cease to appear. Could this be the event prophesied at Fatima? Only time will tell.

FURTHER ADVENTURES WITH MARY

Upon returning from Medjugorje, I hit the road again, this time to give talks and to show the DVD filmed for our band of sixteen pilgrims. One night about twenty-five women crammed into the living room of a friend in Virginia. At the end of the evening, a woman approached, introduced herself. It turned out she was the minister who took the photo of Mary at the early Coptic Church in El Zeitoun, Egypt that was given to me by my Mt. Shasta Mary's Garden friend. I just had to laugh. The minister presented me with fifty smaller copies of the same print to give away in my travels at no fee. This could not have just been coincidence.

The next stop was a visit with friends at their home in western North Carolina. Mary had always been a primary topic of conversation between us. Our spirits soared as we spent yet another evening in story swap. I told them about my trip to Medjugorje, then, about meeting the minister who took the photo of Mary at the Coptic church in Egypt. They were familiar with that photo. Quite naturally our time together evolved into their showing me documentary film footage of the apparitions of Mary in El Zeitoun, Egypt, where Mary first appeared on Tuesday, April 2, 1968. She materialized almost nightly for the next three years then stopped in 1971 when the government decided to sell admission tickets. The documentary shows Mary descending from above as a brilliant ball of light that materializes into her recognizable form as she lands on the roof of the early Coptic Church.

Mary's appearances at El Zeitoun were timely. Relations between the Islamic and Christian communities had dangerously deteriorated. During the three years of apparitions, millions of Christians and Islamic people saw her with their naked eyes. Regardless of faith tradition, miraculous healings of the blind and disabled occurred, many medically documented. Without doubt, Mary's intervention thwarted the serious violence that was ready to erupt.

Next, I headed west from North Carolina. The adventures with Mary continued. Before leaving the area of the Yankton Sioux Indian Reservation in South Dakota, I had planned to visit the Cultural Center. Instead, I wound up at the Catholic Church where a delightful nun and I swapped titles of books on psychology, and a volunteer asked for information about Medjugorje. I gave away five of the El Zeitoun photos. One nun who received a photo yelled out of her car window as she drove away, "Who are you, anyway? Mary is my patron saint!" We laughed as she sped away. There is much joy and fun along with the serious message that Mary brings.

A month or so later I arranged to go on retreat at Christ in the Desert, a Benedictine monastery northwest of Santa Fe, New Mexico. The dirt road from the main highway is seventeen miles long. It was springtime. It had been raining. It was mud season. New Mexico is famous for the car-sucking mud that will stop your car dead in a ditch faster than a sneeze. Anyone who lives there knows. I stopped at a Ranger Station to check my directions and to get a mud report. The Ranger looked out the window at my car when I told him my destination. He said, "If I were you, I wouldn't attempt it." Later on down the road, I stopped for gas, asked the station owner the same question. Same answer. "I wouldn't go there if I were you." Okay, now what? I decided to press on. Wherever I wound up was wherever I wound up.

Heading north towards Chama, I began to notice signs for a wool-spinning and rug-weaving cooperative called Tierra Wools. Oh, dear, I intuitively knew my unseen friends wanted me to stop there, but I just was not in the mood to visit a wool shop. Having worked hard to unload all unnecessary physical possessions, I surely did not want to purchase anything. So I chose to be in a state of resistance and limitation in my expectations as to the purpose of the wool shop stop. Suppression of the nudges worked until a larger-than-life prairie dog ran into the road in front of my car at the exit for Los Ojos and Tierra Wools. He was enormous … and extraordinarily bold. Courageously that prairie dog stared me down while standing upright on his hind legs. I had been clipping along at a good rate of speed in my determination to go anywhere but there. To avoid hitting him I swerved off the highway onto the road that angled down into the one-street town. It was not hard to find a parking space in this nearly deserted old west town.

Full of beautiful loom-crafted historical style rugs made from local grown and dyed wool, the shop was actually interesting. The women behind the counter were engaging. Quickly we dove into conversation about the ongoing history of relationship between the local tribes and the first generation Spanish who moved into the area at the time of the conquistadores. They shared their vision of the store as a cooperative designed to support local sheepherders while keeping alive the endangered art of loom rug making through their rug-making school. Somehow, I wound up telling them about Medjugorje. The visit was enjoyable, but the full reason for stopping there had not yet made itself known. I had the familiar anticipatory feeling that gives way only when the puzzle pieces have locked into correct position. There was nothing else to do but continue to hang around until that lock-in happened. The women asked where I planned to spend the night. They encouraged me to stay at lodging connected with their business. Since Christ in the Desert was no longer an option and I was out in the middle of nowhere with dark gray skies auguring an incoming storm, their suggestion seemed reasonable.

Once settled into the lodging, I took a ride up to Chama to fine dine at Subway. Boy, it was gloomy at that little winter dead-to-tourists town! After returning from dinner, it was time for a walk. Beckoned by a light bulb burning brightly in the distance, I walked up the hill to see what was there. To my amazement, what was there was a beautiful replica of the Lourdes grotto, complete with Bernadette looking up at Mother Mary. A local family who adore the Holy Mother had constructed the little grotto. The puzzle pieces flew together instantly. I was surprised the women at the store had not mentioned the shrine since we had talked about Mary. It seems that reminders of Mary's constant presence exist just about everywhere!

Here's another one. One Easter Monday, after visiting in New Hampshire, I drove southwest into the Berkshire region of Massachusetts to the lovely town of Stockbridge. This is a stately community of well-kept residences and majestic trees. After having a brief look-see, I thought it time to get back on the highway to continue the several hours trip to my next destination. What happened next was odd. I just could not find the way out of town. Something was up. I was the clueless one. The interstate was close by, but its entrance remained elusive to me. To clear my head and frustration, I decided to park the car and take a walk. I had no inclination at all to stroll along the store-lined main street. Up the hill looked physically stimulating, so that was the way I went. Soon I noticed a large campus on the left, then a sign for the National Shrine of Divine Mercy. Guided to this enormous Marian retreat center, I had arrived just in time for the Easter Monday 3:00 p.m. mass in the beautiful little campus chapel. Afterwards I returned to my car and found the interstate entrance with no difficulty.

I have been pushed, shoved, and cajoled off the road for one reason or another in spite of myself. The inner delight experienced each time is better than the best bakery cream-filled donut! I fill up with a sense of wonder and joy.

On a beautiful summer day in 2007, I drove south from Denver on I-25. I prepared to make the cut over to Ft. Garland and then head on down into New Mexico. A perfect cloud formation likeness of the U.S.S. Enterprise, as in the *Star Trek* television shows and movies, appeared in the sky. Accompanying it were two smaller scout ships. It seemed they were going to lead the way so I followed as they traveled ahead of me. As we approached the magnificent Mt. Blanca, they turned north towards Crestone. I love Crestone. It's like Brigadoon, a mystical, imaginary Scottish community that can only be accessed once in a hundred years. When the timing is right, you can enter into Crestone, home to numerous spiritual retreat communities that take advantage of its remote mountain location.

On the way in, I checked the community bulletin board for lodging for the night. To my surprise, the name of my Mt. Shasta Mary friend was listed among the bed and breakfast owners. Well, another Mary day it surely was. I called her and arranged to spend the night. One night turned into two nights of happy reunion. A realtor as well as a healer, my friend wanted me to see a listing in her neighborhood. It was a multi-tradition retreat center. The owner, a lover of Mary, Buddha, and Native American teachings, had constructed a perfect miniature adobe chapel, steeples and all, to honor Mary. Beautiful and welcoming, the sanctuary can accommodate four people comfortably as they sit upon prayer cushions. The altar centerpiece is an exquisite, elegant, enlivened wooden carving of Mary. Special thanks went to my friends on the USS Enterprise for reuniting me with this good friend who has been an integral part of the Mary story of my life. The two of us enjoyed sweet meditation together in the energy of The Mother.

A few years ago, after completing a teaching engagement just east of Buffalo, New York, I headed south. North Carolina was my next destination. I angled off I-81 at Harrisburg, Pennsylvania, in order to connect with I-95 via Route 15 because it offered the most direct connection between the two. I grew inexplicably, overwhelmingly tired just south of Harrisburg. Too tired to drive safely, I got off the road to register at the first hotel in sight. It was pricey but, to my delight, the manager gave me a "manager's special rate." Happily, I sunk into the luxurious bed and slept like a baby all night. Fatigued from having been on the road for several weeks, I was tempted to stay another night. When I asked the next morning about the availability of another "manager's special," the hotel clerk was shocked. He said they did not have such a thing. The night of luxury was over. I had been the recipient of a thoughtful gift, reason yet unknown; it was time to move along. I just said a thank you, tally ho and back on the road, Joe.

Not far down the road, a sign pointed to the entrance to the National Shrine of St. Elizabeth Ann Seton. By now quite interested in the lives of the saints, I headed in. The basilica was stunning. The volunteers were like angels—full of love and quite willing to answer questions. I knew nothing about this obviously important woman. A volunteer explained that Elizabeth Ann Seton was the first American to attain sainthood. Born an Episcopalian in New York City in 1774, and of high social status, while in Italy with her sickly husband, she had a profound religious experience that resulted in her conversion to Catholicism after his death. Peers and family members, appalled by her decision, shunned her. The Catholic Church placed Elizabeth in Emmitsburg, Maryland, where she established a school for girls. She also established the first branch of the Sisters of Charity in the United States, an affiliate of the Order of St. Vincent de Paul. Her story is an inspiring one. Mother of five children, the doggedly determined Elizabeth left her world of wealth and comfort to serve people in need in the religious tradition that spoke most clearly to her.

St. Elizabeth Ann Seton's remains lie beneath the Altar of Relics in the breathtakingly light-filled Basilica. Colorful mosaics behind the altar depict the Blessed Mother as she appeared to Catherine Labouré. Aha, here was another story to learn. Catherine Labouré, born in 1806 on a farm in the town of Fain-les-Moutiers, France, had been devoted to Mary since early childhood. When she was a young teen, she dreamed one night of a priest who told her, "God has plans for you."[7] A few years later, Catherine saw a painting of the priest from her dream hanging on the wall at the Daughters of Charity facility at Chatillon-sur-Seine. He was St. Vincent de Paul. She decided that she wanted nothing more than to become a Daughter of Charity. Although her father did his best to dissuade her from her purpose, eventually she wore him down. On Wednesday, April 21, 1830, Catherine entered the motherhouse of the Daughters of Charity in Paris.

On Sunday, April 25, 1830, the visions of Mary began. First, for three days in succession she had visions of the sacred heart of St. Vincent de Paul. She also had begun to have regular visions of Jesus, but kept this a secret. When she began to doubt the accuracy of her perception, the visions of Jesus stopped.

Catherine had prayed since childhood to see Mary. On July 18, 1830, she had a feeling that Mary would appear to her that night. At 11:30 pm, an ethereal male child awakened her. He urged her to go to the chapel. He said that the Blessed Virgin awaited her there. Mary did indeed appear to Catherine in the Chapel. Catherine was permitted to place her hands on Mary's knees. Mary talked about difficult times that were to come and where to find consolation during those times. She also told Catherine she had a calling, a specific job to perform.

During a second vision of Mary on November 27, 1830, Mary asked Catherine to have a medal made to be worn around the neck; those who wore it and had faith would receive great grace. This medal is the renowned Miraculous Medal, known and cherished by Catholics worldwide. The story behind the medal's creation remained a secret until after Catherine's death. Now I, too, knew the story behind the medal that appeared among pieces of fruit I was considering purchasing at a produce stand in Sydney, Australia, winter of 1998. Another mystery solved!

The day at the Shrine was not complete. I went into the store to look around. Two women were present, a helper who stood behind the counter and an elderly nun. The nun left for lunch. This left just two of us in the store. Quickly we dove into deep conversation about all kinds of matters to do with Mary and Jesus. While we were talking, a book fell off the shelf seemingly by itself. The book explained common rituals of the Catholic Church. I bought it. Then, having established that I frequently visited Rhode Island, the helper asked if I had visited the home and gravesite of Little Rose Ferron. I listened with rapt attention to what the docent shared about Little Rose, victim soul.

Little Rose Ferron was born on May 24, 1902, on a farm in St. Germain de Grantham, Quebec. In 1905, her family moved to Fall River, Massachusetts. About this time, Little Rose began to experience states of religious ecstasy. Her health began to deteriorate, but her love for Jesus only increased. The family subsequently moved to Woonsocket, Rhode Island. The strange illness kept Rose bedridden. In 1926, the stigmata — the wounds of Christ — began to appear on her body. First the whiplash marks, then wounds to her hands and feet, then the imprint of the crown of thorns around her head; eventually her eyes shed blood. This occurred every Friday for one year beginning in August, 1929. All of this was documented by priests and medical people who visited Little Rose in her home. On August 1, 1930, outward evidence of the stigmata disappeared, although her internal suffering continued each Friday.

Little Rose's home became a place of pilgrimage. People traveled from all over to receive favor from Jesus through Little Rose's prayers of intercession. Many of them reported miraculous healings. Little Rose died on May 11, 1936, at the age of thirty-three. Reports of miraculous healings through prayers to Little Rose continue to this day. A devoted group of believers has made appeals to the Catholic Church to beatify and grant sainthood for Little Rose. Many official documents compiled during her lifetime and submitted to the Archdiocese of Providence, Rhode Island, have been unfortunately lost. This fact, of course, has made the beatification process a difficult one. The phenomenon of Little Rose has been the subject of highly charged church political controversy ever since application was made for sainthood.[8]

I was unfamiliar with the concept of the victim soul, a soul or person divinely chosen to suffer more than most people and who accepts this suffering in order to be close to God. Little Rose, once a seemingly healthy child, was bound to boards to keep her limbs from overly contracting. She suffered greatly. I found it hard to comprehend why any soul would choose to suffer this way. Perhaps it is to demonstrate that we are not the body. Her ecstasy was a spiritual ecstasy that appeared to transcend pain. I wondered if I would have the courage to bear what Little Rose and other martyrs have endured. I wondered about the strength of my faith. Would I stand up for God no matter what? Little Rose's story also turned my attention back to Fall River. Before Little Rose's family moved to Woonsocket, Rhode Island, they lived in Fall River and worked in the mills.

PART FOUR
RED FLAGS

ENERGETIC RESIDUES

Mother Earth had been the focus of attention during much of my travels. Travel, travel, travel, often without clear conscious knowing as to why I am directed to a country, or to take one certain route over another. Once I get to the target destination, what usually comes is a flash of awareness followed by a deep dive into residues telling of events that took place often a very long time ago. Since 1997, I have come to know other people who work and travel in this way.

Several years ago, I headed to Florida. Traveling south through North Carolina, South Carolina and on into Georgia, I awakened as though from a trance. The road was unfamiliar. Deep, uncontrollable sobs burst out for no apparent reason. I drove another half hour, all the while sobbing. The source of the deep soul-connected emotional state was unknown until signs for Andersonville began to appear. I knew about Andersonville. This was an ancestral as well as a collective sob. My paternal great grandfather was a prisoner at that hellhole from which a monstrous number of Union prisoners of war did not emerge.

Andersonville was a death camp. It was filthy. The water for Union prisoners was deliberately sewage-degraded; there was not enough food; housing was makeshift tattered tents for those so fortunate. Thousands of wounded and ill soldiers were packed into the site. Under such adverse conditions thousands died from disease and unchecked lawlessness. Andersonville is now a national monument for all American prisoners of war. I found my great grandfather's name on the prison rolls. I walked the grounds that day, and have subsequently driven all the roads that jut forth from and around Andersonville. The roads are radii that pour forth into the surrounding region the sustained pain of the atrocity of war to which Andersonville gives ongoing testimony.

All events leave energetic markers. This is why we feel happy and content in some areas, confused and unsettled in others, downright creeped out with an urgent get-me-out-of-here impulse in yet others.

In early December 2007, having left Prasanthi Nilayam, Puttaparthi, India, main ashram for the avatar Sathya Sai Baba, it seemed important to visit a lake in the large city of Hyderabad before catching a return flight to the United States. My friend and I arrived at our hotel at four a.m. after a twelve-hour train ride. The desk clerk at the hotel cheerfully said, "You must go to visit the giant Buddha statue in the lake while you are here." Sai Baba's portrait smiled down from the wall behind him. Bingo! Specific location provided through the clerk, compliments of Sai Baba. After a short morning's sleep, we traveled with our Indian friend to visit the enormous statue once blessed by the Dalai Lama. On the way, she explained that the park we would pass through to get to the boat that would ferry us out to the Buddha statue had been the site of a terrorist bombing on August 25, 2007. Two terrorist attacks took place that day: one at the park, the other at a food establishment. In total forty people died. The site needed healing prayers, as did any souls who might linger.

Another place that provoked deep unease is the town of Rock Springs, Wyoming. I pulled into town to find lodging for the night. Because the area felt disturbed, I asked the hotel manager about the history of the town. He said that Chinese railroad workers were massacred in Rock Springs on September 2, 1885. The Union Pacific Railroad Company had brought in Chinese laborers at lower wages than they had been paying to white immigrant laborers. Racial tensions mounted alongside the economic distress. Twenty-eight Chinese miners were murdered, fifteen injured, and over seventy of their homes burned. Prior to registering at the hotel, I knew nothing about the history of Rock Springs. Over the years, I have learned to seek out what I can about the history of an area when experiencing this kind of unease.

One day I will not forget was my visit to the site of the Civil War Battle of Chickamauga, Georgia, recorded in the annals as one of the bloodiest battles of that war. The fighting raged for three days, from September 18 to September 20, 1863. Apparently, all the animals and birds went silent from the ungodly noise. I didn't know about Chickamauga until noticing the sign while driving by. Once there, I surely felt the horror of all the killing. My reaction was so physical I thought I was going to die. Somehow, I got back to my car to call a friend for help. With her long-distance assistance, I regained enough strength to drive away. I have wondered since how the people who live in that area fare, what their state of physical and mental health is, what the rate of depression is, and whether the area has high statistics for violence, depression, and suicide.

The Sand Creek Massacre site, located in eastern Colorado, is another. I went in purposeful search of that location, but did not find it. At the time of my attempt, the site was not included in the travel guide for the State of Colorado. Furthermore, there were no apparent signs in the vicinity. For a couple of hours, I drove all around the country roads— agri-business territory and home to cattle research ranches. Finally, I stopped a farmer who was navigating his giant-wheeled harvester across a field. As soon as he jumped down from the machine, he asked me if I knew how to protect myself from attack. That was odd. He showed me a technique to use against anyone who attacked from behind. I took that warning seriously. The area was a bit unsettling. I asked about the massacre site. He asked if I'd come for the meeting to be held the next night to decide if the massacre site would become formally recognized and made into a National Monument. He said the site has been "disturbed" ever since the massacre, and that white farmers had no success on that land ever since the massacre. I was not there for the meeting. I knew nothing about it. However, I was glad to know it was happening. Public recognition of this tragedy was necessary for true healing to be accomplished.

The Sand Creek Massacre took place on November 29, 1864. Black Kettle, Northern Cheyenne Chief, and Chief Niwot of the Arapahos had taken their people to camp along the Sand Creek after traveling to nearby Fort Lyon to make a declaration of peace. Times had been very difficult for native people with the continual breaking of treaties by the United States government and the frenzy of the Gold Rush that brought money hungry miners and settlers.

As instructed, Black Kettle had raised an American flag above his lodge in the encampment. The US government told him that the raised American flag would protect them from aggression. However, the Territory of Colorado had a clear policy of extermination against all Indians. Here is a quote from Colonel John Milton Chivington, US Army and Methodist minister, who led the massacre: "Damn any man who sympathizes with Indians! ... I have come to kill Indians, and believe it is right and honorable to use any means under God's heaven to kill Indians."[9]

I will not go into the horrifying details of the massacre. It was the ungodly, unprovoked, and deliberate murder of peacefully assembled people, purportedly in the name of God who said, "Thou shalt not kill."[10] What a terrible misuse of religion to justify rapacious, greed-driven conquest.

Finally, the Sand Creek Massacre National Historic Site, located in Eads, Colorado, was officially dedicated in 2007.

Countless prayers, spirit, and earth release work has been and continues to be offered at places like Gettysburg, Wounded Knee, Andersonville, the Sand Creek Massacre, the Twin Towers. Too many sites like these exist all over the planet. Areas of untended historical trauma bleed through to attract and generate even more disturbance and mayhem in macabre magnetic action. We must realize that everything we think, say and do flows outward like proverbial ripples on a pond into and onto the world in which we live. We carry these memories in our bodies that are made of the Earth. We carry these memories from other times and places in our soul bodies. We carry these memories through ancestral thought field and genetic transmission. Geographic areas that lack harmony can trigger us into states of energetic, emotional disarray. Unaware, we can absorb and perpetuate that impacting imbalance in some way.

You might be feeling right about now that I am overemphasizing the negative. That is not my intent. Each of us carries distinctly positive memories of times we have spent at the beach, hiked through a lush rainforest, or witnessed a field of colorful flowers. We do not need to redress such experiences. It is important to savor the positives, to remember that moment of felt oneness, to immerse in the beauty of this planet. However, there are areas and historical circumstances where the wound needs to be exposed and prayerfully, energetically cleansed for proper healing to occur.

Pope John Paul II apologized to the world during his papacy for two thousand years of wrongdoing by the Catholic Church. The Australian and Canadian governments publicly apologized for the atrocities perpetrated against the indigenous people of their nations. Aboriginal people had been waiting for this for far too long. Such public pronouncements do make a difference. While the facts of the past are unchangeable, honest, sincere acknowledgment helps. During our lifetime, we have even witnessed the bringing together of veterans from nations who fought against each other during World War II. This is healing for those veterans in ways that people who have not had the experience of war cannot understand.

Often enough I have watched people squirm with obvious discomfort when they come face to face with the harsh reality of our nation and our planet's past. They wonder what their responsibility is in this time and place for actions perpetrated by ancestors and people they never knew. What will right the undeniable wrongdoings? Acknowledging what obviously happened is a good place to start.

The Battle of Little Big Horn Battleground site, situated in Montana, expands the idea of respectful acknowledgment. Once a monument solely for the US military, this site has become a monument for both Native American and US soldiers who died in that military engagement. Since childhood, I had struggled to keep my anger in check regarding the atrocities inflicted upon the native people of North America. Visiting Little Big Horn helped to put things into better perspective. Each grave marker for the US military tells a little about each soldier who died: his age, where he came from. Many were immigrants newly arrived who entered into military service as a way of starting life in a new country. This information gave form and substance to the deceased for me and stimulated a sense of compassion I had not previously felt. The compassion allowed me to forgive them. The recently completed Native American memorial sculpture purposefully opens toward the monument for the US military to honor those soldiers who died. This is the concept of All My Relations at work. I thought of Father Svet's concern about why monuments exist. The Battle of Little Big Horn monument now acknowledges that military engagement in a balanced way.

Years ago I traveled the Trail of Tears in reverse, meaning that I began the route in Tahlequah, Oklahoma, and followed the trail back to Cherokee, North Carolina. Marcellus Bear Heart Williams, a Muskogee Creek medicine man and friend, sent me off in a prayerful way. The journey filled me with a terrible sadness along with horror that my government had deliberately perpetrated this death march upon the Cherokee, Choctaw, Creek, Seminoles, and Chickasaw people. The Indian Removal Policy of the United States government was all about the great land grab. By the time I arrived at the well-done native museum in Cherokee, I was fierce with emotion. A gentle, kind Cherokee elder named Jerry Wolf greeted me at the door. He stayed with me as I tore through the bookstore picking up books about Sitting Bull, Tecumseh, Crazy Horse, Geronimo and other great Native American leaders—my heroes.

Jerry Wolf's response to my angst was to sing "Amazing Grace" in Cherokee right in the middle of the bookstore for all to hear. His singing was heartfelt. As he sang, my anger dissipated. When he was done, I asked how he and his people could move beyond the tragedy of the past. He picked up a book written in Cherokee and pointed to the letter that started each sentence. He said it meant, "Here, now." What a teaching.

I have never forgotten Jerry Wolf. I thought then and still do that these native people, torn from their long-established communities, were far more "Christian" than those who ordered them onto that genocide trail. First degree murder has nothing to do with the teachings of Jesus.

If we cannot forgive, how can we truly heal? Denial and holding onto ancient and not-so-ancient anger, sadness, grief and trauma drags us down as you have seen from my story. I have received multiple teachings about the importance of forgiveness—of self and of others. Forgiveness is essential. Also essential is that we not repeat the behaviors that give cause for acts of repentance and forgiveness.

NATURAL DISTURBANCES

I had hightailed it out of Fall River almost as soon as its ravaged skyline loomed into sight from the highway. Something in me knew ... something. My body recoiled, contracted. The first thought I had was that the people of Fall River had lost their connection with Mother Earth. Everywhere I looked I saw cement.

Mother Earth provides the material substance for our physical bodies as she does for all creations of the physical world. Our physical senses and consciousness so intricately interwoven with her massively larger life-giving feminine body, we are literally wrapped in her. The all-encompassing consciousness of the Absolute infuses her just as it does all living things. We live on and in her body. She, Earth Mother, lovingly shares of herself so that we can, as spirits, take on physical form.

When we cut ourselves off from Mother Earth, we are only half connected. Residing in her body, we feel what she feels. She feels what we feel. Sometimes we sense that something is missing, even if we cannot define it. That is why restorative time in nature, away from high-rise buildings, technology, macadam and cement, is so important. In uncompromised nature, reconnected to the mother energy, it is possible to regain a sense of oneness, peace, and spiritual renewal. We thrive in balanced mother-father energy. When disconnected from true nature, what we do, say, and think goes askew.

I sensed that part of the problem with Fall River had to do with the cementing over of her body in that community. Cover-ups do not work. They implode. We have witnessed this implosion with the disclosures about long-concealed sexual abuse. Harmful secrets rarely remain secrets. The risk is greater not to address the wounds that fester through secret keeping.

Recently I happened upon this excellent statement by Terry Tempest Williams in her brilliant book, *Finding Beauty in a Broken World*: "Our kinship with Earth must be maintained; otherwise, we will find ourselves trapped in the center of our own paved-over souls with no way out." In typical Williams' style, her non-fiction storyline juxtaposes our wanton destruction of every living thing with the afflictions of the human species. She draws a parallel between the longstanding genocide perpetrated against prairie dogs and the genocide in Rwanda. The consequences of our grievous disrespect cause catastrophe for all species and ecosystems of our planet.

The depth of human-earth relationship was emphasized during my last, quite strange camping experience in Grand Teton National Park. Previously, camping there was an enjoyable event. On this occasion, it was not. I had looked forward to pitching my tent in this region of spunky mountains that independently jut assertively into the big skies of Wyoming. This night, however, was not to be one for quiet reflection and soothing connection with the earth. People were noisy all night long. Park rangers yelled and banged on the doors of a nearby camper at three a.m. It was bizarre. Exhausted and irritable, I went into meditation with my guides for explanation about the strange goings on. I was shown the interior of Mother Earth, how her tectonic plates, as they shift and grate upon each other, create instability that impacts human behavior as well. They reminded me that Yellowstone National Park sat due north.

I knew geologists were becoming concerned about increased volcanic activity in the great caldera beneath Yellowstone. I remembered the call for specific prayer work for Yellowstone by Bennie Le Beau, Shoshone elder, to address the problems there. From the indigenous point of view, the area had become unstable due to the blocking of ancient prayer ceremonies that helped maintain balance. Now the disturbances of the night made sense. Mother Earth and we are so connected, yet we seldom consider this fact.

The message from the Teton experience was further expanded four years ago when I traveled to New York City to facilitate healing for a woman who suffered physically, emotionally, mentally, and spiritually. We had worked together before. In a constant state of upheaval, she had a difficult time keeping her head above water. As I stepped out of the elevator onto the floor of the high rise where she lived, my body swayed in a disorienting way. I felt somewhat spaced out. The sensation was strange, and had never happened before. As I began to work with the client, my guides showed me the source of the elevator experience. Manhattan sits directly on a fault line that runs down the east coast of the United States from Maine into New Jersey and beyond. My client's apartment building happened to sit directly on top of this fault line. There was activity along the fault line that very day; that was why I felt the way I did. Furthermore, my guides said that it would be a challenge for some people to maintain health and well-being in this particular location because the disturbances in Mother Earth affect even the cellular structure of the human body.

Astonished, I shared with the client what my guides revealed. She said that many of the people in the building developed health problems not long after moving in, that health issues went with living there, that the issues generally diminished upon relocation to another area of the city. This experience provided another opportunity to understand the delicate relationship between Mother Earth and us. The understanding gained of course did not fully explain the client's difficulties—she had a history of disturbances that long preceded her taking up residence in that particular apartment building. Nevertheless, the shifting in Mother Earth's body further compromised her health. Once again I was awed by how much there is to learn.

When we are in an aware and respectful relationship with Mother Earth, we have a better chance of knowing how to proceed. Stories abound, past and present, from indigenous cultures about listening to the wind, meditating with fire, observing and learning from the behavior of the creature beings, sitting with a tree as a way of gathering life-sustaining information. The animal kingdom, attuned to subtle shifts in environment and frequency, knows to evacuate areas of earthquakes and tsunamis long before most humans notice that something is happening. It seems that the more "civilized" we become, the less conscious we are. For the most part, we've lost our connection with nature. And the less conscious we are that everything that exists is in relationship, the more disrespectful we become. Revelations that come from quiet time in nature have been lost to the credo that more noise and busy, busy, busy is best. Most humans are unaware of their ability to receive the messages that are gifts transmitted through openhearted relationship with Mother Earth, the plant realms, the creature beings, and the mineral realms.

A wonderful teaching story emerged from the tragic tsunami of December 26, 2004. I heard it first during an informal gathering with His Holiness Gayuna Sundima Cealo, Buddhist monk, and then again when it appeared on television news the next day. The story was about the water nomads, an indigenous people who live in the country of Myanmar. They are boat people who live life happily, simply, and in continual contact with the spirits of nature. Some of the nomads sensed on the day of the event that something was not right. The water did not look right. The tsunami had not yet hit the coastline of Myanmar, was not visible, but it was on its way. Because the nomads had never lost their direct relationship with the natural world, because they were engaged in ongoing communication with the spirits of nature, they had the information they needed to save themselves. They knew that they had to get as far away from the shoreline as possible. Those that did survived. The life-saving awareness came through their connection with nature. An interesting point made during the television interview with nomads who survived is the fact that they do not have words in their vocabulary such as my, our, your, and theirs—they have no concept of ownership and material possession.

One thousand year cycles exist that have great influence upon the people of this planet and the planet herself. This is common knowledge in the inner sanctums of religious and spiritual traditions worldwide. Every one thousand years the "demons" resurface and must be dealt with. Unleashed, these minions of the dark must once again be "put down" by those who specialize in such work. When this eruption happens, all hell breaks loose—literally. The disturbances that ensue create mayhem inside and out. War, violence, and chaos erupt. Undercurrents of depression, anxiety, inconsolable grief, seething unseemly hatreds, and ancient vendettas burst forth like a plague infecting humanity. We witness a dramatic rise in the number of suicides and homicides. The energies work their perfidy from the unseen realms to disturb body, mind, and spirit. What I am sharing here is not a secret: it is currently the "hot" subject of a multitude of books, television shows, and movies. The evidence is everywhere in the dramatic deterioration of morals and values and the disregard for the sanctity of life. At the end of the cycle, with the dissembling of the world of opposites, one thousand years of relative peace is destined to ensue.

However, there is even more to know about the time in which we have chosen to live. Not only is the thousand-year cycle erupting upon us, we also are completing a larger cycle of time. Native people would call it the end of the Fourth World. Hindus call it the end of the Kali Yuga: a 26,000-year cycle during which we have been farthest from God. John the Evangelist wrote about this time in the Book of Revelations. As we tumble down the chute into the riotous rapids of this stupendous, momentous, amazing time, everything and anything that has not been properly tended to within and without is being brought to our attention for redress. An apt analogy is that the entire planet and all people are in God's great washing machine for the ultimate cleanse. We live in a time of great opportunity. The washing machine is loosening 26,000 years of residue so that we can shed it to emerge all bright and shiny—as individuals, communities, states, nations, and as a world.

We have choice as Frodo has in *The Trilogy of the Rings* by Tolkien. The path at the end of his journey was a hard one, but with Sam as his friend, he completes his grueling, life-threatening mission in spite of the all-alluring tantalizing pull of the dark. Tolkien wrote this trilogy about the human race's great dilemma after personally experiencing the horror of World War I. J. K. Rowling's wildly popular Harry Potter series addresses the same quandary. Harry Potter, the star student, stands out because he calls a spade a spade. Fearless, he says what others are afraid to say. He confronts what others are afraid to confront. He does what needs doing, all the while having the grandest, most thrilling adventures.

In truth, each of us is Frodo, Sam, Harry, Hermione, and all the other great characters in these stories. Like them, we struggle our way through, relying often on the honesty and support of trustworthy friends. What way will we go? Will we resist the temptations of greedy evil? Will we choose love? Will we fall back into old patterns that take us down into the abyss? You can well imagine our friends of the Light and those of the dark are waging bets behind the scenes right now. The spiritual bookies are having a heyday! It is all quite fascinating.

Do not forget for a moment that the choice about which way to go is an individual one. Which way do you choose?

In the early 1930's, the local priest, Father Bernardin Smoljan, and his parishioners wanted to erect an enormous cross on top of the mountain named Krisovec to commemorate the 1900th anniversary of the crucifixion of Jesus. The added hope was that with dedication of the site the ferocious hailstorms that pummeled the region would stop. The Archbishop of the Diocese of Mostar forwarded their request to the Vatican. Pope Pius XI was stunned when he received the appeal. In 1932, he had a vivid dream of climbing an unknown mountain. During the dream, Miriam (Mother Mary) visited him and said, "I want you to build a cross on this site, because this place will become very important in the future." When the Pope saw the photo of the site proposed for the cross, he recognized it as the one in his dream. He sent money immediately to fund the project along with an actual piece of the cross on which Jesus was crucified. He instructed that the piece of cross be placed in the center of the enormous structure.[11] Next, an architect designed a magnificent cathedral capable of holding far more people than the population of the region dictated. The cross and the cathedral set the stage for what was to come in Medjugorje.

Obviously, something is working behind the scenes in places like Fall River and Medjugorje. The question is who and/or what. Simultaneous with the apparitions in Medjugorje were apparitions of Mother Mary in Rwanda. Her message to a handful of Rwandan schoolchildren was similar to the messages given to the Bosnian visionaries. She warned of a terrible time of genocide to come.

It appears that a timeline is in effect, that someone or something knows ahead of time of what is to come. Most times when Mother Mary appears she comes as prophet. A good read about Mary as visionary is the book written by former CIA agent Ingo Swann, called *Great Apparitions of Mary: An Examination of Twenty-Two Supranormal Appearances*. In the case of the El Zeitoun apparitions, bloodshed was averted through Mary's ministry from the rooftop of that Coptic Church. Protection enveloped the community of Medjugorje because parishioners followed Mary's instructions. The area just outside city limits tells an entirely different story.

Rwanda has its own miracle stories. *Left to Tell* by Immaculee Illibagiza shares the story of how she and seven other women survived what would have been certain death from genocide. Hidden for three months in a tiny bathroom at a pastor's home, they dared not speak lest the killers hear their voices. The space was so small they could not all stand or sit at once. During this terrifying time, Immaculee could hear her would-be murderers calling for her through the walls of their hiding place. Immaculee now travels the world teaching forgiveness. She also is actively involved in the creation of the Shrine of Our Lady of Sorrows in Kibeho, Rwanda, where Mother Mary appeared to three young women between 1981 and 1983. Her messages presaged the genocide to come.

Not only Mary is at work to encourage humanity to come back to solid relationship with God. The prophecies from a myriad of traditions — Hopi, Cherokee, Incan, Mayan, Tibetan, and more — remind us to put our spiritual connection first. They warn about the very disturbances we are currently witnessing. They remind us to be respectful of all living things and to live in balance with nature. We have guidelines to follow that ensure a more peaceful, harmonious existence — if we would follow them. When we forget who we really are, that we are beautiful spirits all come from the same source and that there is enough for every living thing, we become greedy. Greed and fear of not having enough gets us into big trouble, causing serious distress for every other living thing, including Mother Earth.

In 1985 the focus of my life shifted when I was thrust into an intense and ongoing period of soul-level healing related to specific people and events from this and other lifetimes. The gift of the healings with my birth parents brought me into deeper relationship with Mother-Father in the larger sense of the word. The reconnection with the God I have known by many names across millennia is now well established. For this, I am eternally grateful. However, the pursuit of absolute truth while following the clues deeper and deeper into the larger historical picture led me to wonder if somehow we humans are being forced to follow some kind of bizarre *Robert's Rules of Order* in a game that is more complex than we know.

One day I protested mightily after listening to an audiotape of Homer's *Iliad* during a long drive down I-95. It was obvious that the humans in this famous story about the ancient battle of Troy were merely disposable pawns on the chessboard of the gods and the goddesses of that time. The humans had no free will. That really made me mad. Immediately I experienced the sensation of being physically slapped upside the head by the Greek goddess Pallas Athena. That was a shock. I have trusted her through lifetimes and she does this to me? Her message: this is the scenario and I just needed to get a grip. Say what? Clearly, the stakes of this "game" go beyond the human experience. She was teaching me something that day that took years to comprehend.

The masterfully crafted storylines upon which we have based our reality are so well done that we have stayed within their confines for ages. The stories are in literature, mythology, religion, art, film, and the oral storytelling traditions from the most ancient of times. We have lived in the most committed way to these stories. We have believed wholeheartedly. We have been raised to believe in war, conquest, we/they, dominance/submission, that there always will be those who have and those who have not. The list of constructs to which we have subscribed is quite long. Well, maybe it is just time to cancel this subscription! Maybe it's time to move out of Plato's Cave and onto the Divided Line with our sights set on the enlightening Sun.

The theme of the Jim Carrey movie, *The Truman Show*, is that Truman has a big wake-up moment. He realizes that he has been living fiction, that someone or some collective has taken great effort to keep him unaware that there is something more. Sure, he has a relatively comfortable life. But it just isn't enough anymore. The urge to go beyond what he has known is unstoppable. Truman unlocks the door to the Cave and walks out of the movie set. With determination, he takes himself beyond the storyline that had confined him. Another movie on this theme is *The Matrix*. Keanu Reeves as the character Neo wakes up and, with great effort and some exceedingly speedy and talented help, embarks upon the Great Escape. He has to learn fast, has to train, and work hard to break out of the world that had enslaved him.

Distractions purposefully designed to keep us mired in a state of forgetfulness and the story of the moment bombard us continually. Drugs, alcohol, sexual and other addictions poke holes in our energy bodies. These holes allow disturbed energies to come into our bodies to influence our thoughts, emotions, and behaviors, now from the inside. We also contain self-created energies that backfire on us through thoughts and emotions that we have nurtured and cultivated to the point that they take on a life of their own. Fully dedicated to arousing our carnal senses, these interferences from within and without urge us to engage in behaviors that actually are not normal.

We are now seeing evidence of such behind-the-scenes provocation in homes and communities all over the globe. People who have been abstinent from all sorts of addictions are having inexplicable relapses. Violence to self and others is dramatically on the upswing. The unseen influences drive right on into those in-between spaces of our quantum bodies to attack our psyches and emotions. Most humans are unsuspecting targets. One way to maintain control over a group of beautiful souls is to keep them enslaved in the excesses of the material realm. We have become slaves to the god called "More is Better". We are proud of our possessions, not knowing that we are the ones being possessed.

This may seem to be the stuff of science fiction, but it is not. Upstanding human beings who love and help one another generally do not think and behave in unkind, self-destructive ways. It is not normal to inflict grievous harm upon an entire population for purpose of controlling not only thoughts, words, and actions, but also a populace's health and well-being. Something else is at work here, something that has been the subject of stories passed down for millennia and found in film, television, and books of present time. Consider that something to be a collective of controlling non-love energies that no longer even bothers to conceal itself. Furthermore, it cannot. As the veils between worlds thin, as more people wake up to their unadulterated true selves, the ones who wish to maintain power and control at all cost simply cannot hide.

BEYOND FEAR

Now is a good time to talk about fear. We each have our moments of apprehension. I have surely had my fair share. What is important is not to allow it to dominate. Once you have had your fear burp, get back into center. Be proactive. Intend to realign with Mother-Father God from the Source beyond all Sources. Anchor yourself firmly in the earthly body provided courtesy of Mother Earth and your conceiving parents. Send roots down into Mother Earth's central crystalline core to stabilize yourself like the mightiest of oak trees. Give all your fear up to Original Source—all of it! Call upon the mighty Archangels and the innumerable ministering Angels who love you and wait for you to ask for help. The non-love energy wants nothing more than to keep you in a state of fear, anxiety, lethargy, hopelessness, and helplessness. Do not cooperate. Give the fear up. Rise beyond the programming to connect with the love that is always emanating from Source. If you have difficulty believing in God, believe in the goodness and power of love. You know love. You know how you feel inside when you love without stipulation. This is not a lusty love. This clear, unconditional, non-seeking, comfortable, comforting, generous, heartfelt love brings serenity and peace.

Stay with this line of thought, please, bizarre as it may seem. I may have really rattled some cages. Good! We are coming to the end of that 26,000-year cycle called the Kali Yuga, which means we are getting into position to move into the return path to God. We are in the time of the prophecies, all of which point to this momentous moment in time and tell us to get back to basics, get our priorities straight. The Fourth World of Duality, the time of colliding polarities, is ending.

According to the ancient prophecies that Gram taught, the First World ended in ice, the Second World in fire and the Third World by flood. Every culture has a story about The Flood. That something will happen as the Fourth World concludes is inevitable. One way or another, the particular world in which we live will end through some kind of planetary event, some kind of shift in consciousness. We are truly in the thick of it now with unpredictable weather patterns, volcanic eruptions and earthquakes, war and more threats of war, chaotic human behavior, global economic instability and irresponsibility, and manmade environmental disasters. Disturbing as these events are, they are indicators that we are approaching what comes next: the Fifth World, a world of unity, a world of balanced masculine and feminine, a world of peace and enough for all. Let us do our inner work with our eye on that desirable goal.

What we most need to be concerned about is the integrity of our soul. Do we capitulate to the energies within us and around us that want nothing more than to distract, oppress, and perhaps even steal our soul? This is possible through further blind embrace of unchecked materialism, lust, greed, and disrespect for Mother Earth, maltreatment of one another and other species, acts of war, and disregard for the sacredness of all life. This is possible if we do not do our inner housecleaning with courage and care. What do we believe in? Where do we find true balance and comfort? Let each of us choose to go beyond the parameters of what we have known.

Thousands of years ago I gave too much of myself in an attempt to save my friend who had become "the devil incarnate." I "sold" my soul to Mephistopheles in the naïve and mistaken belief that I could prevent my friend from falling deeper into evil (non-love). This action cast me into the Realm of Lost Souls. Yes, such a place does exist. I was taken there consciously once in 1997; it was quite sad to witness all the suffering souls who were confused and trapped in that horrid abyss. Retrieving this aspect of my soul has been quite a project. Because the path is full of all sorts of temptations, distortions, and distraction, my choice is to stay as alert, awake and discerning as possible so that I do not fall backwards. I almost succumbed to that black magician's skillful efforts to suck me back down. I was naïve, too trusting, too curious to suspect the purposeful weaving of that malicious web around my consciousness. In truth, the entire episode was a spiritual test to see if I would stand in and for the Light.

There is no more time for head in the sand ostrich naïveté. We really do need to have our wits about us. That being said, I cannot emphasize enough how much help we have, how loved we are. The dramatic, sometimes physical incidents of my life have been attention getters as well as reassurance that I am not paddling solo. I have learned to ask my spirit helpers to "Please give it to me three different ways so that I don't miss the message!" I call this the Law of Threes. Much help comes from our physical family, birth and otherwise, as you have seen through my stories. My birth mother acknowledged the circumstances of my birth … and apologized. My father helped me heal from that ancient time of smashing while incarnate and, more recently, from the other side. White Waters and Grandmother Twylah would not let me off the hook—I had to take responsibility for myself, had to get honest. Mother Mary has been helping me to heal and love myself. Following her deftly laid out itineraries, I have learned a lot about the history of this planet, its imbalances as well as its beauty, and especially the unshakeable love of the Mother. Ever searching for absolute truth, Mary's guidance and wisdom have been instrumental to this quest.

Faith and trust have deepened for me through living the experiences that have flowed steadily since 1985. Fear, anxiety, and feelings of separation dissolve each time I surrender to God. Stabilized in the boundless love that shepherds me from the spiritual dimensions, I really do know that all is well.

The following three stories further demonstrate how up close and personal our spirit teams actually are. Such assistance truly abounds for each one of us. The first event took place in 1996 in northern Ontario at the completion of an action-packed seven-day women's wilderness canoe trip. The trip was a great success. The finale was incredible. Satisfied after a well-earned dinner, we sat around the campfire to enjoy our seventh and final night of camping. To our utter amazement, wolves began to howl. The sound traveled across the lake first from the south, then from the west, finally from the north. It was almost total surround sound. To dowse our skepticism, for no one had reported the presence of wolves in the area, coyotes began to yip, a dog barked, and loons warbled their curiously strange songs. No doubt about it, we were hearing wolves. The experience was humbling, primal, and encouraging. When we arrived back at base camp the next morning, we reported our auditory encounter. Our greeters were not convinced until another group of canoeists following us in told the same story.

After the participants departed by float planes, I returned to the mainland by barge. Full of gratitude for this once in a lifetime experience, I contentedly retrieved my trusty Ford Blazer from the parking lot of the marina. I began the long drive home on the dusty, little-traveled six-mile dirt road that would dump me back onto the main highway. About halfway, the right rear tire blew. I waited a while, hoping for help, but not one person drove by. I had to change the tire by myself, something I had never done before. Just as I was completing the task, a small compact car with a young male driver slowed on approach. He drove past, stopping a short distance away. He sat in his car a while, then slowly got out and walked toward me. He said nothing. I had a bad feeling about him, but did ask if he would put the ruined tire in the back of my car. I kept my back against the car, eyes fixed on him at all times. The thought in my mind was that he could do anything to me, kill me, toss me in the woods, and no one would ever know. All my senses were on red alert. The next thing I remember is that I was driving quickly down the road toward the highway, doors locked, with dust kicking up behind the car, young man nowhere in sight. I know that I received divine help that day, help that probably saved my life. While I did not see my helper, I believe that my guardian angel reached through the veils to intervene in an undeniable, physical way.

The second event took place between six a.m. and six forty-five a.m. at Oakland International Airport one week before the United States invaded Iraq in 2002. My trusty friend had dropped me off at the terminal in a timely manner. I stood in line with everyone else, looked at my watch, noticed who was near me in line and who was standing at the check-in counter. Forty-five minutes later, I and two other persons standing nearby came to, as if we had emerged from a trance. We looked at our watches. The time was six forty-five a.m.. Surprised, we affirmed for each other that something unusual had just occurred. Not one person had moved in the line. The same people were standing at the check-in counter. This was definitely a "stopped-time" incident. Passengers for other flights had been moving past us the entire time. However, for us, time had stopped, then restarted as we hustled to make our flights. Quickly checked in, I successfully ran to the plane. My baggage did not fare so well; it arrived the next day.

Well, what was this all about? I went into meditation with my guides for answers. I had been worrying about the consequences of the United States invading Iraq. The stopped time event provided reassurance that something would be done to protect us—humanity—from ourselves if we stepped too far over the line. My guides reminded me about the 1973 intervention that occurred, with witnesses, at the F. E. Warren Air Force Base in Wyoming. The base housed missiles in silos during the 1970's. Sentries reported to their commanding officers that UFOs were hovering over the base. The UFOs proceeded to disarm each of the missiles one by one.

I understood. I was to stop worrying, was to trust more deeply in the assistance that is ever-present for our troubled planet. Because everything we do has an effect upon the entirety of our universe, we require monitoring.

The experience was comforting, particularly since it followed a visitation from Archangel Gabriel on a cloudless, beautiful, California clear blue-sky day. My friend and I were about forty yards away from her house, started out on a walk, when a lightning bolt slammed down onto the pavement in front of us. Shocked, we ran back inside, went into meditation, and learned that Gabriel was telling us to pay attention because the next step in the Armageddon process, the invasion of Iraq, was about to take place.

The final story shows what good listeners our spiritual helpers are. The following occurred during the John of God event at Omega Institute in Rhinebeck, New York, on September 29, 2009. I was sitting in deep meditation as a volunteer medium during the afternoon healing session. For some reason, I grew concerned that there was not enough spiritual assistance present in the room where I sat. I put out a silent call for help. Later I was to learn that I was not the only person asking for more healing presence. Immediately, the Entity incorporated in Medium Joao rose from his chair in the next room. He walked through all the meditation rooms, passed by those of us seated in the front row in the room where I sat, then returned to his seat. After the session, I found a voicemail waiting on my cell phone. It was from my eighty-two-year-old friend who lived in Connecticut. She was responding to the voicemail she said that I had left for her earlier that afternoon. I had not called her. At least I had not thought I had called her. When we spoke that afternoon, she said that my voice came onto her voicemail, and then, faded out as another person left a voicemail. Was I okay, she asked? Did I need help? We giggled over the fact that she heard my call. At dinner that evening, a staff member from the Casa pointedly asked if I was okay. Yes, I said, emphatically and with a smile, I was definitely okay. So just in case you wonder if you're being heard when you put a call for help out into the spirit realms, let this story reassure you. I have laughed so many times, and with the deepest of gratitude, for this wonderful experience. Take it from me—our helpers really do hear us!

CHANGE

Succumbing to the temptations that abound in the material and astral worlds is far easier than staying surefooted on the path of return. The latter requires steadfast spiritual discipline and determination. Giving in to self-destructive urges is old pattern capitulation to desires that are not true needs. We know this path well. We have traveled it for a very long time. The consequence of continuing to follow that same old path with its deeply carved ruts, however, is not to our benefit.

I periodically think about a pivotal book from my post-graduate training days called *Change*, written by Dr. Paul Watzlawick. Simply put, Dr. Watzlawick states that we have two choices in times of crisis. We can achieve homeostasis by utilizing familiar problem-solving methods. He calls this "first order change." This is restoration to what was the status quo, a pacification of sorts. Alternatively, we can learn, grow, and go beyond our comfort zone to achieve what he calls "second order change." Second order change sets something new in motion. I love this concept because it speaks to evolutionary change. How appropriate it is for us to actualize second order change during this revolutionary time.

Each day, sometimes each moment, offers opportunities to choose change. When confused or in a state of chaos—inner or outer—we can easily find ourselves sinking down into the moose muck. If you have not had that real life pleasure, I'll define it as deep, dark, fertile, boggy mud with the emphasis on deep and boggy. Moose love to dine in moose muck, hence the name! Humans don't really navigate so well in that environment. For starters, we lack the four extremely long legs that enable moose to move slowly and freely as they joyfully munch their way along. We want to get out of there; it is not in our best interest to stay in odiferous murk that bogs us down. Mucky confusion distracts us away from our main goal, which is to evolve our soul as we seek the return path to God.

When I realize I am confused and have landed in the muck, usually it's because I have cut myself off from Source. To reconnect, I stop what I am doing, get quiet, and set the intention to realign with love while sending roots deep into Mother Earth through the bottoms of my feet. Next, I breathe in and out normally at least three times. In a moment, I am home. I visualize myself held in a tractor beam of love-filled crystalline white light that flows from the farthest reaches of the firmaments down through the center of my being and into Mother Earth. It is like being in an elevator that accesses two floors. The top floor, called Source beyond Source—the Absolute—is the penthouse. The ground floor is the center of Mother Earth. There are no in-between stops. Quickly I find myself in the center of the great universal love that is infinitely available for us all. Flow resumes with this simple meditative act. Answers appear, situations resolve with ease, and all is harmonious again.

It seems evident that the souls residing on this planet have arrived at the long prophesied T-intersection. Souls who have not already chosen have two options: the way of love or the way of non-love. Either way, we change. The path of love inherently begets more love, more compassion, more humility and generosity, deeper regard for the sanctity of all life, deeper peace and inner joy. Persons traveling the non-love path change in a different way. Their love and light dims; their auras darken. The persons we loved and knew, their hearts hardened, grow angrier, blaming, harsher, more critical and miserable. Sharing little in common, heartfelt, open conversation between love and non-love people has its challenges. Some relationships we have enjoyed for years therefore unravel and fall apart because we really have begun to live in two different worlds. The difference in world perspective and experience between residents of the two worlds is remarkable. Fortunately, for those who embrace love, new friendships develop that are nourishing, enjoyable, and identifiable by that sparkle of sunshine in the eyes. Yes, it does take one to know one!

When we witness loved ones falling into the miasma of non-love, we naturally want to help them. There is a limit to what we can and should do we can become energetically compromised if we over give. The dark sucks energy. First, we must take care of ourselves. This is not selfish. When depleted, we become vulnerable. Those who have conscious awareness of their plight, strong discipline, and an absolute commitment to love can regain their balance. The commitment to heal must be one hundred percent, twenty-four/seven, and include a consistent spiritual practice in order to diligently override the seduction and trickery of the inner/outer tantalizers. We cannot do the work for them. We can cheerlead, prompt from the sidelines, but the work is theirs to perform. Living through the experience myself, and having watched more than a few individuals disentangle their souls from grasping energies that would control them, I know that the objective is achievable. Additional encouraging news is that many humans are now having spontaneous awakenings onto the path of love. Traveling across the country and to different parts of the world has allowed me to observe this heartening phenomenon.

During a recent intimate meeting with Native American elders, one elder said knowingly, "We don't even know who is sitting at the dinner table with us anymore." People are changing. None of us is exempt from this volatile time of transformation. We have a choice to make. The time for that choice is definitely now.

Ever since reading Viktor Frankl's powerful book, *From Death-Camp to Existentialism*, later renamed *Man's Search for Meaning*, I have drawn comfort from the power of the human spirit to rise above the most horrible circumstances imaginable. Frankl, a neurologist and psychiatrist who survived the concentration camps of Nazi Germany, poignantly shares his experiences in the camps, his observations about the human spirit, and the importance of finding meaning in all forms of existence. He stated that the challenge is to change ourselves when we cannot change the conditions of our lives. He believed that each of us has a specific vocation or mission in life, that we each have a unique assignment that demands completion. Therefore, each of us is essential; none of us can be replaced; nor can our lives be repeated.

Each of us has a purpose. Each of us has something unique to contribute during our lifetime. We can easily become overwhelmed into inertia if we think we have to take on the task of changing the whole world. That is an impossible task. Changing ourselves, our outlook, our attitude, our behavior—this is not impossible.   Examples of humans fulfilling their missions abound. We have only to consider the courage of Martin Luther King during the tumultuous era of Civil Rights in the 1960's. Think also about Greg Mortenson, author of the book *Three Cups of Tea*, who literally came down off the mountain, K-2, and into the loving care of the people of a remote village in Pakistan.   That experience propelled him into a previously unthought-of humanitarian mission. His organization, Central Asia Institute, builds schools for girls in Pakistan and Afghanistan. Both men allowed the spark within to grow and guide them to do good work in the world. Mother Teresa, of course, is an obvious recent contributor to the betterment of life for millions of people in need.

All over the world are people I call Earth Angels. They may not make the headline news, but to those around them, their efforts make a difference. I think often of Rachel, my surrogate mother. She was a black woman who grew up in the segregated south. Her father was a teacher and sharecropper, her paternal grandmother a native of Cuba. Her father and grandmother left Cuba with the hope of finding a better life in the United States. Rachel's dream was to go to college, become a teacher. This dream was shattered when her mother died during childbirth with twins. Because her older siblings had to work in the fields, she had to quit elementary school to take care of the babies. Eventually she married and moved to the northeast.

Fortunately for us, my parents hired Rachel for housekeeping and childcare.   In spite of the adversities of her life, Rachel loved us unconditionally. Her faith in God was unshakeable. She never complained. She never talked about her past. She never thought about herself. Her attention was completely upon the health and well-being of her own family, our family, and countless others. She gave her life for all of us. Her family was one of two black families to live in an otherwise all-white middle class town. That took courage, for racism was abundant and the norm. Rachel lived to the age of ninety-one. Her funeral service, conducted by four ministers, was inspiring and heartfelt. People cried, "What are we going to do without The Mother?" Yes, Rachel embodied the essence of The Mother. Larger than life, she fulfilled her mission of love in the humblest of ways.

When we show up for ourselves, for our friends and families, if we are generous, kind and loving, that is good enough. We do not have to be famous. So many humans truly are Earth Angels who humbly go about the business of loving and watching out for the people in their lives. I believe that the everyday people are the seed carriers for peace. There is no reason to be discouraged. Drink deeply from the all-sustaining deep well of love within and move forward in change with grit and purpose.

A POWER GREATER THAN

An aunt's funeral kicked off one amazing day. My sisters, daughter, and I piled into the Chevy Blazer for the familiar trip to our hometown. We made good time until just before the turnoff onto the country road that would deliver us to the funeral home. Somehow we wound up on a road that was not part of our route, had to backtrack, all the while worrying if we would arrive on time. We raced into the funeral parlor just before the memorial service began. My youngest sister, daughter, and I went up to the casket to pay our last respects. The three of us watched in awe as something subtle, something breath-like, shimmered just above the physical body of our aunt. We were seeing our aunt's soul!

When it was time to drive from the funeral home to the cemetery, we piled back into the Blazer. I started the car, put it into forward, but it did not move. A great unseen but physically felt force blocked all movement. We looked at one another in astonishment. We all felt the power of that force. Confounded, I turned the engine off. We sat a few moments, and then decided to try again to join the line of cars that was exiting the parking area. This time the car moved freely, as though nothing strange had happened.

After her burial, family and friends gathered at our aunt's home for a visit. Late in the day, my sisters and I turned to a discussion of dreams and meditations we recently had. The focus grew laser-specific as we realized that a precognitive warning had come to each of us, separately, without consultation, about a particular cousin. The information given was identical. She would fall during a rock-climbing outing and die. Shocked, we knew that we needed to deliver the warning. Certain that the message would be received with skepticism, we nevertheless carried out the responsibility we had been given. I am pleased to report that this cousin is alive and well today.

Despite feeling sadness about the loss of a favorite aunt, the funeral began a day filled with spiritual presence and presents. Through direct, shared experience, each of us received affirmation that while the body dies, we do not. We felt the presence of something greater and all-powerful. Finally, we took from the day a renewed appreciation for the loving support that watches over us from the realm of spirit. All we need to do is to be open, listen, and allow.

SATAN DOESN'T COME FOR LOVE

Some have encountered a presence that is at the same time enchanting and terrifying. Those of us who believe in the power of love have the tendency to assume that everyone, including a presence commonly called the Devil would want to heal in order to have a greater experience of love. I am here to tell you that this is not so.

I heard an excellent account two years ago from a well-spoken, wise South American woman. A government office worker, one day she felt ill and thought it best to return to her apartment. As she got into bed, she noticed a reddish glow enter her living quarters near the door. A charming, incredibly handsome, well-dressed, elegant man stepped out of the glow. Tantalized, she opened her heart to him. Then, in a moment of absolute clarity, she realized that he was Satan. Wanting to help him heal, she decided to send love to him from her heart. His response was to shape-shift into the familiar figure of Satan with horns and tail. Horrified, the young woman recognized the impossibility of sending love to something that does not want to receive love. She proceeded to pray with all her might. He disappeared in a poof from her apartment.

If something like this happens to you, command and demand that energy right out of your world. You have the right to do this. Call upon Jesus, Mary, Buddha, Archangels Raphael, Michael, Gabriel, and Uriel to remove the uninvited energy. Recite the prayers and mantras that you prefer. Ask your Divine Self and your Wonderful Team to come in closer around you. Every day I ask Archangel Michael to guard my back. He does! Sometimes he reveals his presence through the smell of chocolate. Then I get hungry for cookies and cake. Please regard such encounters as moments that provide teachings about what goes on in the unseen realms. When the student is ready, the teachings and teachers do appear.

Many years ago, just after my first vision quest, a friend said she could not stand to be near me, that I was full of too much joy. Chronically depressed, she said being around me hurt her. She told mutual friends that I needed medication because I was too happy. Our friendship gradually ended as we grew farther apart. On a separate occasion, someone close to a family member told me she could not bear to be in my presence because it hurt. Suffering from severe addictions, she said my presence showed her where she was not. This was excruciatingly painful to her. These two incidents were surprising as well as educational. Not everyone will respond positively to the increased joy that comes from soul awakening.

In the beginning, I wanted to share my renewed zest for life and broadened perspective with everyone. Having jumped into the grandest puddle of love, like an exuberant puppy, I wanted everyone around me to do the same. A slow learner, eventually I came to appreciate that each of us follows a uniquely tailored path that unfolds according to an individualized and ordered timing. Now I do my best to be respectful toward others. It is not for me to judge anyone. I will speak the truth, as I understand it, when asked to share information. I try to remember to say, "Do you really want me to tell you? If what I am saying is more than you choose to hear, you need to tell me that you have heard enough." This seems to work out well for everyone.

Ordinarily I would not repeat what I am about to tell you. However, the ramifications of the debate that is currently taking place truly goes beyond all religious and spiritual structures. Recently I happened upon comments by a former chief exorcist for the Vatican that Medjugorje is of satanic origin. I discovered his comments while reviewing the history of Medjugorje on the web. The link to the commentary popped unbidden onto my computer screen. Shocked, I followed the link, which, unfortunately, I can no longer find online to offer to you. I had no idea such controversy raged publicly amongst high-ranking priests and laity of the Catholic Church. Their debate propelled me to revisit a bizarre post-Medjugorje experience. I had begun to feel "driven" by something that increasingly irritated me when I would recite the Lord's Prayer and the Hail Mary. The prayers would drone on in my head endlessly without relief. The feeling was most unpleasant. It felt as though as I was psychically dueling with some kind of a presence that seemed to be riding in, on, or under the prayers.

During the spring of 2007, as I drove cross-country from the Southwest to the East Coast, I decided to stop once again at the Cahokia Mounds, the ancient city and ceremonial site previously mentioned. I loved visiting Cahokia, had visited there five times prior to this particular day. On this occasion, I could not find the exit for the Mounds, and not for lack of trying. After circling around and around for the proper exit without success, I exited the highway to ask for directions. I went into three different businesses—in Cahokia. No one seemed to know about the Mounds, let alone how to get there. How curious. Frustrated, I drove back onto the highway for one more unproductive try. Cahokia obviously was not my destination of the day. Blocked from going there, I unhappily surrendered to this apparent fact. Then a sign for The National Shrine of Our Lady of the Snows came into view. Without doubt, this was my destination. A beautiful center that honors the Holy Mother, the complex has shrines for Fatima and Lourdes and a lovely garden dedicated to Our Lady of Guadalupe.

On any other day, I would have been more appreciative. This day I was plain irritated. It felt like I was being controlled and in a way that was not positive. My inner dialogue with the opposing energy went something like this: "I am *not* going to join the Catholic Church. I'm too old to be a nun. I would not want to be one anyway because I would have to give up my life's work and my freedom. This lifetime has been all about being out in the world rather than remaining cloistered in monasteries and motherhouses. What do you want from me?" I yelled inside at the top of my lungs. With this, a cord snapped. I felt it. Initially surprised, the next feeling was relief. I realized instantly that a mind control program that I had not even known existed was the source of the grating beneath the prayers. What a very sneaky business. As a result, I really did not know what to think about Medjugorje.

The sorting out process took almost two years. What was going on in organized religion? When I felt the cord snap, I also saw cords running below the surface, in between the lines, through all the religions and systems of the world. The vision was faith shattering. Simultaneously, other "truths" began to unravel. The world as I had known it once again tumbled upside down, inside out. This led to confusion about what and who to believe. What is the absolute truth? What is lie? The journey ever since has been intense, sometimes shocking, and quite surprisingly grounding.

Some of you may reach different conclusions about this particular experience. Some would say that I was being called to join the church and that the internal irritation came from not acquiescing. Some would appropriately wonder if my experience was an outcome of visiting Medjugorje or a visit to some other holy or unholy site. Maybe the control sneaked in from somewhere else. Maybe it was inside me all along, waiting for the appropriate time to surface. Perhaps the insertion took place during an especially challenging meeting that included a few Inquisitor-like individuals—the dominant energy in that particular meeting was definitely not from the field of love. Maybe it had nothing at all to do with any of the above. The range of possible sources is extensive, and all are up for valid consideration.

Whatever was the original cause for the above, that experience underscored my belief that mind control does exist, that we have arrived at the very situation that the Russian scientists feared. Such programs are woven through all societal structures with great artistry and stealth. The programming is not limited to religious institutions. It is technologically imbedded in the entirety of our communication systems—cell phones, digital television, computers, cell towers, iPods, to name the primary venues. As lambs led to slaughter, we have no choice but to utilize these otherwise excellent systems for work, recreation, personal financial transactions, communication, and for keeping updated on world and local news. Let us choose to be judicious in how we utilize the above technologies.

I know this sounds sci-fi, the stuff of fiction. We do live in bizarre times. However, what I have seen and experienced in tandem with unsolicited reports from others who are similarly aware affirms such a conclusion. The evidence is everywhere. The mind control programs also go beyond technological infiltration, like what happened to me. We cannot dismiss the mind distortions that come from interference by discarnate, remote-viewing, and other unloving energies that work diligently to keep us from liberating ourselves. Remember, too, that some are thoughts, beliefs, and emotions that have been self-created, then energized to take on a life of their own within our hearts and minds.

Mary has been shepherding me for many years now—outside the confines of structured religion. I believe that she, as universal mother who cannot possibly be contained or claimed by any religion, helped me that day through the cord-snapping incident to understand more about the pervasive controls that run in-between the lines. She even took me to one of her sanctuaries to accomplish this task.

As for my having a solid relationship with Mother-Father God, this is not even a question. I can feel this relationship directly no matter where I am and what I am doing. The connection is in my heart. Whether I am chanting in the mandir at Sathya Sai Baba's ashram in Puttaparthi, India, meditating beside a lake; sitting in the presence of His Holiness Sundima Gayuna Cealo, visiting with the Sufi Imam at the Islamic Mosque of Jesus the Christ in Ephesus, Turkey, or simply sitting in the stands of a sports stadium on a sunny fall day, I can open up to have the same wonderful loving presence flow through me that is God as I know God to be. Therefore, I do not feel any need to go searching for what I already have found. God is everywhere, in everything.

This chapter would be incomplete without some simple, practical suggestions. Keep your energy high, your heart, mind, and eyes focused on God, on love, on the positive. Keep your inner/outer environment clear, balanced, and energetically secure, your body as fit and healthy as possible through exercise and authentic organic food. Reduce, drastically, your reliance on technology for entertainment and communication. Turn the television off. Put the cell phone away from the body, out of the bedroom, especially away from babies and young children. Limit the use of cell phones as much as possible. Stay out of the continually broadcast toxic news, emitted endlessly through grim reaper, fear-based, repetitive news reports. Most of it is designed to make us upset. Why go there? If you believe in the Law of Attraction, that like attracts like, you would probably prefer to attract something other than fear. Fear begets fear. Love grows love.

Read good books. Spend time in nature. Play games that are fun and that build relationship through shared experience with family and friends. Resurrect the ancient art of storytelling. Instead of communicating by text messages, how about having live, face-to-face visits? Human beings have somehow managed to live for thousands of years without being tethered night and day to cell phones and computers. All of a sudden, we seemingly cannot bear disconnection.

Sounds like the Borg from the television series *Star Trek*, to me. The people of the Borg function as one mind through imposed technological hookup and programming that constantly monitors each individual to disallow independent thinking. We do not have to become Borg. Choice comes through awareness. Knowledge is empowering. Be proactive.

FALL RIVER AND MEDJUGORJE REVISITED

As you now know, geographic "hot spots" exist where war, massacre, inhuman and non-loving behavior periodically erupt. The Middle East is clearly such a cauldron. I believe that the area of Fall River, Massachusetts, is another, although I cannot tell you the full story—because I do not know it. But it is obvious that this area is troubled. We know about the deliberate slaughter of Native Americans, colonial times, the Revolutionary War, the active slave trade market in neighboring Newport, Rhode Island, the devastation to near extinction of the right whale population by the whaling industry out of New Bedford, the Industrial Revolution, and the burgeoning disclosures about sexual abuse in the Catholic Church. Are these surface symptoms that point to something else that lies beneath the surface?

Interesting clues that I have intermittently pursued are twofold. New England is repository for what appear to be Druid structures, of which America's Stonehenge, located in North Salem, New Hampshire is the most outstanding. I highly recommend the book *America B.C.*, by Barry Fell, to begin to stretch your ideas about the pre-colonial history of North America. The Druids were active on both sides of the Atlantic. The Royal Society in London knew about this particular site, and, in fact, was actively engaged in research that stopped when the Revolutionary War began.

Next, physical evidence testifies to visitation by Templar Knights to North America over one hundred years *before* Columbus. After leaving the port of La Rochelle, France, in 1307 to escape the Inquisition, the Templars sailed to Scotland, reputedly carrying the substantial treasure that had been stored in their Paris temple. With Henry Sinclair, well-known Templar, they traveled to Nova Scotia, Vermont, Massachusetts, and Rhode Island. Discovered in Fall River was an unusual suit of armor that is Templar in origin. Columbus used Templar maps and charts to "discover" America.[12]

Verrazano's voyage in January, 1524 was for the express purpose of locating the Templar colony. He found no Templar Knights, but he did find physical evidence of their presence along the shoreline of Newport, Rhode Island. People who live in Newport are familiar with the twenty-five foot high rounded baptistery, still standing, built in traditional Templar style. Did the Templar Knights escape to North America with something that the Inquisition wanted? If you want an intriguing read, obtain a copy of *The Lost Colony of the Templars* by Steven Sora.

It is logical to conclude that knowledge existed in the "Old" World about the "New" World long before Columbus's famous "discovery."

Why was this knowledge suppressed—and by whom? Currently, far more questions than answers exist. That there are secrets is undeniable. Mary's deep concern about the Fall River region is striking. What an interesting name for a city.

The region comprised of Bosnia-Herzgovina, Serbia and Croatia—the former Yugoslavia—is another historically disturbed area. Some of the puzzle pieces fell into place when I read James Twyman's book, *The Secret of the Beloved Disciple*. Twyman recounts the story told to him by a Catholic priest named John. The story is an involved one that begins in June 1389 with the Battle of Kosovo. Mother Mary promised a great spiritual gift prior to the battle to Tsar Lazar through a visitation by her intermediary, the prophet, Elijah. If the Tsar chose spiritual victory over material victory, strife between the ethnic and religious populace of the region would cease. Tsar Lazar, a deeply devout Christian, chose spiritual victory. The victory would involve a great sacrifice—his life, the life of his king, King Murad, and the lives of all their troops. Agreeing to win the spiritual victory, the Serbians lost the battle to the Ottoman Empire. Populated by Christians and Muslims, the region thereby benefited as promised through the spiritual victory and went on to achieve world renown as a bastion of peace, respect and multi-cultural cross-pollination.

Nonetheless, the divisiveness born of radical nationalism festered and finally overpowered the grace wrought through the Battle of Kosovo. An ancient curse was purposefully set in place by a dark brotherhood that sowed the seeds for atrocious ethnic hatred and conflict. The Battle of Kosovo became a distorted symbol for Serbian nationalism and patriotism. The Catholic priest privy to this information accompanied Twyman to that region in order to perform specific ritual peace work to offset the curse.

In 1989, the President of Yugoslavia, Slobodan Milosevic, made an impassioned speech to a great gathering of Serbians during the 600th anniversary of the Battle of Kosovo, just two years before the genocide began. This is important from a historical perspective because World War I began after a Serbian nationalist assassinated Archduke Ferdinand in Sarajevo on June 28, 1914, the anniversary date of the Battle of Kosovo. The unaware assassin was front man for a secret Serbian occult terrorist organization called "The Black Hand." World War I became the staging ground for World War II and its atrocities. Thousands of religious Yugoslavians died at the end of World War II, massacred by their nation's military as they returned home. More recently, we have witnessed the 1991-1996 Serbian genocide of over 200,000 Muslims, with over 20,000 bodies unaccounted for, two years after Milosevic's speech.

The information provided through James Twyman fit. I already knew through my travels that dark art magicians have been busily working their craft all over the planet as part of the larger plan of the dark. Yes, it made sense that something else was going on behind the scenes and beyond the awareness of those who travel to Medjugorje and other places of pilgrimage to take advantage of people while they are in innocent states of religious ecstasy. You see, the Light is a magnet for the dark just as the flame is to the moth.

FURTHER THOUGHTS

Exposed to the workings of the dark ones through personal experience, I know how easy it is for unsuspecting people to fall prey to the machinations of those who would manipulate, maybe seek to entrap your soul. The movie, *Revenge of the Sith*, sixth film in the *Star Wars* series, provides an excellent depiction of how the fall happens, as well as how those who are committed to doing dark deeds work. This is the story of the insidious seduction of Luke Skywalker's father, Darth Vader, by the evil Sith Chancellor, Palpatine. The Sith was a dedicated master of the dark; he had neither room nor time for love in his constitution. Obi Wan Kenobi saw the deception, but Darth Vader, emotionally imbalanced, upset, and needy, was blind to the allure of the Sith's false promises. Darth Vader forgot what he had learned from Obi Wan Kenobi. Emotionally distraught, he lost his balance, neglected to protect himself. Vulnerable, he fell. Palpatine overtook him with ease.

Places of healing, churches, temples, synagogues, ashrams, funeral homes, hospitals, battlefields, cemeteries, and disaster areas are ripe areas for contact with confused earthbound souls and other non-love energies. All over the world, millions of people travel to holy sites in search of healing from physical and mental infirmities. Some consciously seek release from known demonic possessions and discarnate attachments. Earthbound souls and non-love energies like to "download" into such sites. Visitors who are unaware of the need to self-protect can "receive" those energies quite innocently. Add in the work of mind control programs, dark magicians, and ancient or current curses whose purpose is to block the love and light of the Supreme Presence and you have a set up for activity that runs in-between the lines all over the place.

Developing awareness that such happenings can and do occur is the first step in preventing such downloads. In recent years, the media has done a great job of exposing the unsuspecting public to some of what goes on behind the scenes through books, movies, and television shows. Fascinated readers and viewers are learning about earthbound souls who have not gone to the light, aliens, vampires, ghouls, all sorts of otherworldly things. The subject stirs up great fear and a sense of helplessness. What is lacking in the curriculum for the masses is a toolbox, a set of protocols that everyday people can use to clear the fear and come back to alignment with God. In the books and movies, hero specialists deal with the problem. Yes, some people absolutely are born preloaded to scout out and intervene. These abilities are gifts of birth. We need these talented individuals. Yet, each of us has what Gram calls latent talents, gifts that we can develop if we step up to the plate of self-responsibility. We all have the capability to create a field of love within and around us that acts like bug repellant. Setting clear energetic boundaries, developing a recognizable, trustworthy connection with our Divine Self, that precious aspect that is directly relating with God at all times, really helps.

Any system that insists that it is *the* way to God has become part of the problem. Any system that insists that it has *the* answers is inherently off-center. How do we know if such systems are clear vessels for truth and love? The same question is applicable to our spiritual teachers and clerical intermediaries. We must become discerning about the structures and teachers we embrace. When independent relationship with God is discouraged, independent spiritual practice condemned, when the directive is that the only way to God is through external intermediaries, the potential for disempowerment is substantial. Ideally, the intermediaries exist only to teach, then encourage those who would learn how to get there on their own. The key concept here is self-responsibility.

Words—read and heard, contemplated and discussed—help to pave the way, but the connection made in the heart and in the bones is what becomes deep knowing. If that connection comes through Native American teachings and the natural world, that is wonderful! If it comes through serving the homeless and hungry, so be it! The priest I met in Fall River before I traveled to Medjugorje believes at an entirely different level because he had an inner experience that produced profound inner knowing. He, like the rest of us, did not know what he did not know until he had an experience that taught him from the inside out.

Please let us not place limits on the avenues for connection with Source. Through wilderness experiences, indigenous ceremony, moments of meditation, ashrams, mosques, temples, synagogues, churches, and spiritual centers like Medjugorje and the Casa de Dom Inacio, millions of people are renewing their relationship with God. The opportunities for moments of God-knowing are boundless because God is everywhere in everything.

Many people receive healing—on occasion, miraculous healing—in places like Medjugorje. Sometimes the process of healing brings to the surface conditions that are pre-existing, situations that have lain dormant or unknown whose time for redress has come. This is the chaining process discussed earlier. Many of my stories demonstrate how this layered continuum of soul healing works. Consider these moments as deeper opportunities for refinement. Rather than judge, just do the work. That the occasion has presented itself is a good thing. Understand that in God's great washing machine for this time, the laundry list is a long planetary and personal one. None of us is exempt. Having arrived at the long prophesied T-intersection, we get to choose the river route our soul will take.

Essential truths, great teachers, spiritual communities and teachings have much to offer that is good. They bring practical inspiration to our world. However, because we as a species have strayed terribly far from the original teachings, evil (non-love) is able to penetrate into every level and structure of our world. Certainly more goes on than meets the eye. Currently the forces of darkness are at work just as they were during the Dark Ages, the time of the Inquisition, and World Wars I and II. Humanity is walking a literal high wire. We have incredible assistance in the spiritual realms, as well as from our incarnate colleagues, but first we have to wake up, show up, and, with commitment, do our part wholeheartedly. When we are spiritually strong, united in community, keep our focus on love and our eyes wide open, we are in good position to ride the waves of change. Remember, knowledge is power!

PART FIVE
RESURRECTION

I arranged to travel to Ephesus, Turkey, in 2006 after awakening in the middle of the night to the most haunting, beautiful birdsong I have ever heard. The unfamiliar melody came from the woods behind my bedroom and lasted one full hour. No one else in the household heard it. In the morning, I asked my spirit guides what kind of bird had been singing. They said it was a nightingale. None of us knew nightingales to be in the region. What was this about?

A trip to Turkey had been on my mind for several years. The urge to go grew stronger after this nocturnal experience though I knew not why. Apparently, it was time. Arrangements fell into place with ease. After three awe-inspiring days in Istanbul, my friend and I traveled to Izmir to meet our Ephesus guide. An archeologist, he revealed that he is a direct descendant of Mother Mary. What an auspicious beginning for our visit to her home! We headed for Ephesus early the next morning.

On the way, we picked up a German woman who left a career in the rock and roll industry the year before to pray every day at this pilgrimage site. As we drove up the hill to Mary's home, our guide mentioned that the name of the hill was Nightingale Hill. Dots connected, I was flooded with emotion. He also told us that a wildfire had ravaged the region two years before. Hungry flames that raced up the side of the hill toward her home abruptly stopped before reaching the top. Changing course, the fire turned back down to burn a path all the way to the Aegean Sea fifty miles away. Obviously, special intercession had taken place, further punctuating the sacredness of this site.

Prior to his death, Jesus had specifically entrusted his mother into the care of John. After his crucifixion and resurrection, because it was no longer safe to remain in Jerusalem, Mary and John traveled to Ephesus where she lived out her final days. When she died, John placed her body in a cave on the property. Three days after her death, her body was gone from the cave, paralleling the disappearance of Jesus' body from the Holy Sepulcher.

The official records of Ephesus document Mary's residency there. This fact is at odds with other information about where she lived and died after the death of Jesus. When I asked in meditation during a subsequent trip to Israel how could it be that two burial sites exist for Mary, my Wonderful Team reminded me that Helen, mother of the Emperor Constantine, had consecrated the site in Israel. One-stop convenient pilgrimage, if you will. The Catholic Church and the Orthodox Church both recognize Mary's assumption (ascension) from the cave on her Ephesus property. In fact, as we traveled from Istanbul to

Ephesus, the Pope traveled from Ephesus to Istanbul. Our guide, who had served as an interpreter for the Pope, told us that an Islamic woman from the area reported having a vivid visionary experience of Mary's assumption. The Pope had hoped to meet with her to hear her story, but the woman, quite ill at the time, died before he could interview her.

Some of the original stone foundation of Mary's home remains two thousand years after her death. The entrance into her L-shaped home led us right into a cozy little chapel where we met Father Mathias, a radiant, soft-spoken priest from India. He asked if we wanted to celebrate mass. We pinched ourselves. In Mary's home? Good heavens! Of course we did! Six of us listened as he gave a wonderful homily that surprisingly happened to focus on the Book of Revelations. It was back to the prophecies, this time the prophecies as recorded by John the Evangelist. I was amazed that Father Mathias chose to speak on this subject. Central to my experiences with Mary has been her continued prophetic messages about our period of history.

Ten days in Turkey turned into a crash course in ancient history. We saw the historic walls of Constantinople, touched the walls of the ancient city of Troy, walked along stone walkways once tread upon by Cleopatra, visited the ruins of the extraordinary Greek healing center called the Asclepion. Surprised, we cried when we unexpectedly encountered the skullcap and right arm of John the Baptist in the museum at the Palace of the Sultans. We toured a room at the same palace filled with articles that belonged to Mohammed. We visited the Blue Mosque, a beautiful world-renowned Islamic holy site, and the Hagia Sophia, once an enormous Byzantine church in part built with goddess-infused columns from the Temple of Artemis in Ephesus and the Temple of Delphi in Greece.

The Temple of Artemis, one of the Seven Wonders of the World, is located in Ephesus. Once a majestic structure that overlooked the Aegean Sea, only one enormous column remains to give testimony to a time when the divine feminine was revered. I have clear memories of this temple. Turkey is also home to sites dedicated to an even more ancient earth goddess named Cybele. Priestesses of this order were highly respected oracles like the Oracles of Delphi in Greece. It was deeply moving to stand upon and walk in places familiar to my soul.

SPIRITUAL RICHES

The quest to achieve a deeper understanding of the plight of humanity, its apparent inability to secure lasting peace, and how to institute viable solutions, has been lifelong. Touring this amazing nation was far better than winning the Mega-Lottery! Turkey is a veritable archeological treasure box that contains layer upon layer of known history—Mesopotamian, Sumerian, Egyptian, Greek, Roman, Christian, Islamic. The sites we visited give tiered testimony to the succession of religions that accompanied occupying civilizations. The occupiers simply built over the existing sites to imprint their belief systems upon the land. This proved cause for contemplation about the longevity of any civilization and religion. One fact is undeniable: underneath all the structures resides Mother Earth. Without her, this beautiful mother, we would not be here, we could not physically exist.

Visiting the home of Mother Mary was central to our journey. Also at the top of the list was our visit to the ruins of the Basilica of St. John, also located in Ephesus. St. John's remains lie buried in this massive religious complex. The holy power emanating from his crypt is indescribable. Sobbing, I was dropped to my knees. In Pammukale, our guide showed us where the body of St. Phillip lies in a sarcophagus, incorrupt. As we sat overlooking the white encrusted limestone thermal pools that strikingly cascade down the side of geologically unique Pammukale, we gazed upon the countryside where the apostle Paul traveled and taught. Paul's letters give multiple references to a whole lot of shaking going on. Many earthquakes happened in that region. The Aegean Sea, because of those earthquakes, is now located fifty miles from Ephesus. Yet the shaking was far more than physical.

From Ephesus Jesus' disciples spread out in all directions to share his teachings of love. Being on actual physical location of this great saga, I was beyond words awestruck by their incredible bravery. All but St. John were martyred. I wondered if I would possess the degree of courage, faith, and commitment required to perform such a daunting task. Each messenger, no matter what tradition, encounters alarming challenges when bringing new thought to the world. Humans prefer homeostasis. When the existing system of belief is disturbed, they seek return to what they have known (first order change). In other words, kill the messenger.

Once a lawyer and rabbi, and directly responsible for the brutal persecution of many early Christians, Paul became a Christian after he had a profound visionary encounter with Jesus while traveling the road to Damascus. Paul's conversion and ministry incensed those in power.

The authorities, some of them former friends, wanted him dead. He shook up the status quo. *Paul and Stephen*, by the Spirit Emmanuel (Francisco Candido Xavier), is quite an interesting account of his transformation and work. Paul is a controversial historical figure, for sure. Yet there is more to him than is commonly known. According to Paramhansa Yogananda, Hindu guru who received many direct teachings from Jesus, Paul was a student of Kriya Yoga or something similar. He was knowledgeable about the science of ascension. He knew how to "die to the body" to travel into the bliss that is Christ Consciousness.[13]

Like Paul, the great Tibetan saint Milarepa pursued a different path after having a profound realization. I unabashedly confess to you that Jetsun Milarepa, whose father died when Milarepa was a young boy, is my favorite Tibetan yogi saint. When greedy relatives stole the generous inheritance left by his father, the boy and his family were left to live in desperate poverty.

His grief-stricken widowed mother, seeking vengeance, decided Milarepa should become a sorcerer. A loving dutiful son, he acquiesced to his mother's wishes. As a sorcerer's apprentice, he learned many things, including "Lung-gom-pa," the Wind Meditation, which is an esoteric way of employing breath to travel great distances without stopping and at extraordinary speed. He also learned the ways of black magic. When he returned to his home village, having learned how to manipulate the weather, he instigated terrible hailstorms that caused the deaths of many people and destroyed their homes and crops. In the aftermath of the destruction, he had an epiphany. Deciding to change his ways, he found his teacher, Marpa the Translator, and after twelve years, achieved complete enlightenment.

Milarepa is reputed to be the first to attain this state of Vajradhara in one lifetime. A wandering monk, he lived in caves, wrote great poetry called the "Songs of Milarepa," and taught both women and men who sought his wisdom. He particularly emphasized the transitory nature of the body and the need to be unattached.[14] During a trip to Tibet in 1999, our group was fortunate to visit Pyenzhangling Monastery in Zhenggang. The monastery encompasses the cave where he once lived. The austerity of the cave that was once his home made real for me his capacity to transcend the body. Though I knew nothing about him before that visit, the story of his life has been a source of inspiration ever since.

The stories of Paul and Milarepa encourage as well as comfort us. If murderers can become loving and beloved, can go on to do good work in the world, so can we. Crucified, we are also crucifiers. Each of us has hurt others as well as ourselves during this and other lifetimes. Early on in my energy healing practice, White Waters nudged me to assist a serial killer to cross over into spirit when he died. Initially I was afraid. However, the fear dissolved with the recognition that, though the killer had lost his way, he was still a child of God who was worthy of loving intercession. Who knows what nefarious deeds each of us has committed over lifetimes. Are we not worthy to receive and to extend love and forgiveness?

CAUSE FOR CONTEMPLATION

Turkey holds an extraordinary and strategic position in world history. Cauldron for a plethora of cultures from antiquity forward, this nation continues to stimulate the mind and spirit. It is impossible to imagine anyone traveling there without being plunged into deep consideration of the successes and collapse of the many civilizations and religions that have preceded us.

The journey deepened my appreciation for the gifts Master Jesus gave the world two thousand years ago. The Apostle Paul speaks to this seeding, this inheritance, in Ephesians 1:11-12: *"In whom also we have obtained an inheritance...who first trusted in Christ."*

Jesus the man first had to develop trust in the Christ. By mastering specific teachings, tests and challenges, he became the Christ. Jesus the man, Jesus the Christ, Jesus the Cosmic Christ. This is the path of the soul as it grows in spirit. This is our path. Jesus teaches us to look beyond the physical body. He teaches us to move beyond the personality, beyond the little "i" that is attached to what goes on in the physical world. Through lessons learned that season our soul, the "i" gives way to the "I," the divine self. When all karmic contracts are completed, we drop our anchor to the physical plane, the soul, and transcend. Jesus planted the seeds of Christ Consciousness. It is up to each of us to water those seeds so that they grow mightily within.

Undeniably, there has been great opposition to, distortion of, as well as blatant misuse of Jesus' teachings. The first heretic martyred in this two thousand-year-old story was Jesus. The teachings he offered would help his followers set themselves free—especially from spiritual bondage. This made him extremely dangerous in the eyes of the authorities. How could those in control contain the knowledge that was spreading like fire? By co-opting, securing, and shaping the teachings to fit their plans through strictly enforced doctrine and structures. We begin to see then the clamping down that has continued, in fits and starts, to this day.

Anyone who deviated from the consolidated religious package organized at the Council of Nicaea, held in 325 A.D., fell into serious, often life-threatening, disfavor with the political religious authorities. The Roman Emperor Constantine, convener of the Council, sought control over the population through the eradication of all other forms of worship by creating one doctrine, one church, one belief system. With the stage set by co-conspiring church and state, the momentum for unbelievable abuse of any individual or community that thought and believed differently compounded over centuries.

One of the first groups singled out for death by the church was the Manichaean community. Mani the prophet, teacher for that religion, resided from 216-276 A.D. in Babylon, which was then part of the Persian Empire. The Manichaean believed in an elaborate cosmological structure. They believed in the existence of two worlds: a good spiritual world of light that was in continual struggle with the dark world of matter. Mani claimed that the earlier teachings of Adam, Zoroaster, Buddha, and Jesus were corrupted. The popular Manichaean teachings spread from the Roman Empire to China. Perceived as a threat to the established religions, the Roman Emperor Theodosius I issued a death decree for all Manichaean in 382 A.D. In 391 A.D., he further declared Christianity to be the only legitimate religion.

Manichaean and Neo-Platonist Augustine of Hippo converted to Christianity in 387 A.D. at the time of the decree. A prolific thinker, debater, and writer, St. Augustine's contributions have shaped the development of the Roman Catholic religion to this very day. The Manichaean perspective on the topic of sin and self-responsibility was particularly interesting to Augustine, one with which he took issue after his life-saving conversion. Manichaean belief was that knowledge was the key to salvation in and of itself. Augustine found this stance too passive and therefore insufficient to effect change in anyone's life. In

Book V, Section 10, of *Confessions*, Augustine has this to say about the Manichaean period of his life:

> "I still thought that it is not we who sin but some other nature that sins within us. It flattered my pride to think that I incurred no guilt and when I did wrong, not to confess it...I preferred to excuse myself and blame this unknown thing which was in me but was not part of me. The truth, of course, was that it was all my own self, and my own impiety had divided me against myself. My sin was all the more incurable because I did not think myself a sinner."[15]

Profound statements on this and other topics abound in his writings. This statement alone is remarkable.

In citing the above, I am attempting to show a bit of the flow of religious thinking since the time of Christ. My journey has been more circular than linear. I have learned that there are parts of ourselves that require reconciliation, and that other things exist that seem to come into us and lodge inside us that do not seem to be part of us. As spirits that drop down from the oneness of The Absolute to take on physical form, what develops during the course of the long journey is the sense that we are each separate from everyone and everything around us. It seems to me that St. Augustine speaks above to the concept that we are all one in the largest sense of the word.

Through the process of spiritual mitosis, the One becomes two becomes four becomes eight and so on, like the physical concept of cellular mitosis taught in biology classes. In this sense, we are all expressions of the original oneness, smaller portions that travel on to have uniquely different experiences. When we as individuated oneness bump into each other, intermingle our subtle fields, we make deposits into each other's energy body. These deposits can affect our inner sense of stability. Downloads that are congruent are noteworthy in that we feel boosted by that which is familiar. Incongruent transfers of energy, thoughts, and emotions often catch our attention differently. We feel out of sorts, have thoughts and emotional charges that are not usual. If we do not notice, those around us do and might say something like, "That's not like you to think (say, do, feel) such a thing." Ultimately, whether these things are self or other-created is unimportant. Our responsibility is to address the matter. Whatever affects us becomes ours to resolve. Therefore, I agree with St. Augustine's conclusion.

As for St. Augustine's concept of original sin, I am not in agreement with the idea that we are born tainted. The Immaculate Conception experience taught me that we arrive into embodiment in a state of spiritual purity. What happens after we get here, the decisions we make, how we behave and think may not be pure, but our spirit is forever pure. Further exploration of this particular concept will have to wait for the writing of the second book of this trilogy. Already I see the threads moving ahead where they await my full attention. There is always something to look forward to in the great mystery called life! Following the clues, as you can see by the various shifts in what has drawn my attention as my journey continues, yields exciting contemplation. Let us return now to the subject under consideration.

Manichaean thinking falls in line with the Gnostic tradition. For the Manichaean, there is an ongoing process of removal of the light from the world of matter so that the light can return to the spiritual world. This idea fits with what I have learned: that we dip down into the physical to have an experience, but that our goal is take all of our essence (light) with us as we exit this world to return to the spiritual realm from which we came. Gnostics, especially the Egyptian-Syrian groups, believe that a remote, supreme monadic divinity exists. From this supreme source, divine beings emanate toward the material realm in a gradual and progressive manner. This process of emanation naturally produces instability in the integrity of the divine. Think in terms of in-breath and out-breath. Initially the breath is strong, but its intensity thins the further out it travels. This lessened intensity contributes to that sense of disconnect with Source that we so struggle with.

What appears next in the descent toward the material realms is a distinct creator God called a demiurge. The demiurge is a lesser, inferior God, a "false" God. In Plato's *The Republic* the demiurge is described as a "lion-faced serpent." The false God is a malevolent tyrant and the cause of all the suffering in the imperfect material world. This demiurge creates a group of colleagues to preside over the material realm and on occasion, to create obstacles that purposefully block those souls who would seek to ascend from the confines of the physical world.[16] This is what I believe Jesus' mission in part speaks to when He encourages us with his words, "Follow Me." He knows the way Home. He teaches us how to bypass those deliberately placed obstacles. I believe that this is what Pallas Athena, my ancient advisor and protector, wanted me to understand when she slapped me upside the head. She was confirming that there are unseen energies that pull our strings.

Now I was getting somewhere. I was finding relevance in ancient schools of thought and teachers that accurately described the understandings I have arrived at through my present time experiences. I ask you to bear with this academic bent just a little while longer. As part of a natural reaction to the kinds of phenomena now presenting across the worlds and dimensions, I had instinctively realized the importance of establishing the God connection to that supreme source—the Absolute, the ultimate beginning of creation that transcends all planets, galaxies and universes and demiurges.

The express intent of the elevator meditation, provided earlier in the book, is to bypass the realm of the demiurge. An appropriate analogy would be cardiac bypass. The new connection, bypassing what is not spiritually healthy and true, goes straight to the heart of original creation. If you believe as I do, we are not the only beings in God's great universe. Something larger than we can wrap our minds around has created all the worlds and universes and the unfathomable numbers of life forms who inhabit them. From this perspective, any attempt to quantify, define and confine what is incomprehensible falls short. The Native American term, "Great Mystery," says it all.

The next story is about the Cathars, otherwise known as the Albigensians, who mysteriously appeared in Europe in the 11th century. Deeply devout, they considered themselves Christians. They followed Biblical teachings, especially those that said not to lie, not to kill, and not to swear. They believed in the existence of a good Creator God and that this God had an evil adversary. They did not have priests, nor did they build churches. They did have an inner circle that conducted ceremonies and worked at menial jobs to support themselves. Cathar men and women were equals. They believed in reincarnation. They practiced contraception. They enjoyed the pleasure of sex without guilt. They were not interested in material acquisition. They believed in the innate incompatibility of love and power. Their numbers grew to include a significant quantity of defectors, including priests from the Roman Catholic Church.

Upset by this state of affairs, Pope Innocent III—what a name— ordered a "Crusade against the Cathars" that was later known as the Albigensian Crusade. He decreed that a Holy Army muster for this purpose. Cistercian Abbot Arnaud Amaury issued the following battle cry when apparent concern was expressed about how to identify who was Cathar, who was not:

"Kill them all. God will know his own."

The genocide that ensued in the region of Languedoc, France from 1209 to 1229 killed over 500,000 men, women and children. This unconscionable military action by the Church, picked up on by King of France, caused the near-extinction of the Cathars and marked the beginning of the Inquisition. The Inquisition continued in full force into the 19th Century. The Office of the Inquisition, euphemistically renamed in 1965 The Congregation for the Doctrine of the Faith, continues to exist.[17]

The discussion would be incomplete without mentioning the Inter caetera, a Papal Bull issued in 1493 by Pope Alexander VI. This document, still on the books and never deactivated, gives unlimited rights of conquest to Spain. Here is a partial quote from the document:

"(that) Catholic faith and the Christian religion be everywhere increased and spread, that the health of the souls be cared for and that barbarous nations be overthrown and brought to the faith itself. We (the Papacy) command you (Spain)...to instruct the aforesaid inhabitants and residents and dwellers therein in the Catholic faith, and train them in good morals."[18]

One year later, in 1494, the Treaty of Tordesillas divided the world in half. Half went to Spain, half went to Portugal. We know the rest of this brutal story. Millions of indigenous people, mutilated, raped, and enslaved, their cultures smashed, died in the deliberate extermination. An effort begun in 1992 by the Indigenous Law Institute to have the 1493 Papal Bull revoked has met with failure. I struggle to understand why; why any religion would seek to grow through massacre, torture, brutal oppression and the establishment of a cult based in fear; why the Church would not choose to revoke an edict that has caused undeniable, unconscionable harm to innocent people all over this planet.

Jesus' ministry was a ministry of love. The Cathar movement, based in love, grew naturally and without force. Nothing good comes from indoctrination through violence—verbal, physical, and energetic—aimed at body, mind and spirit. It appears that someone or something does not want us to live in love. The strong reaction against love proves how wonderfully potent is the power of love. We know that violence begets violence. The crucified become the crucifiers. To break out of this ongoing cycle we must seek the second order change that Dr. Paul Watzlawick discussed. We must take responsibility for our own behavior. Institutions and nations have this same responsibility to come clean, be truthful, make reparation for all wrongful acts, then uphold a solid commitment to the principles of love, integrity, equality, compassion, and respect for all life.

The scenario in which we now find ourselves is extremely complicated, involves worlds and presences beyond the world we think about in everyday terms as home. The quantum field, of which we are a part, allows for movement of discordant energy—let us call it non-love separatist—into and out of the space that we, as individuated drops of the divine, inhabit. The discordant energy seems not to be of us. As previously discussed, we can and do create thoughts and forms that hang out in our subtle bodies. Yes, we do carry memory and manifestations into this lifetime from other lifetimes. Without doubt, the self- and seemingly other-created non-love energies that slide into our fields are our responsibility to expunge through love, whether we like it or not. If we do not take this responsibility seriously, we will find ourselves in deep trouble. The river of change is flowing rapidly now. This river carries debris created since the Great Flood of antiquity. Things are afoot that we have not encountered for many centuries, even thousands of years. The idea of the demiurge makes absolute sense. The demiurge is within as well as without, is internal as well as external. The oppression of humanity is obviously on the incline. We are witnessing an increase in intolerance along with a rise in extreme fundamentalism.

The push to explore differences and similarities in religious belief from ancient times to now has been an unanticipated aspect of my journey. I in no way consider myself a religious scholar. Still, the urge to understand has propelled me in the most surprising directions. The cosmological view that has crystallized for me has developed over time through inner revelation and direct experience, always punctuated after the fact. For many years, I refrained from reading extensively at the urging of my Wonderful Team. An avid reader since childhood, abstinence from books has been necessary in order to learn from the inside out through visceral experience. My Divine Self and guides have been wonderful tutors. We have explored Native American spirituality, the Goddess religions, Hinduism, Buddhism, Spiritism, Shamanism from different continents, Platonic thought, Gnosticism and more. I absolutely believe that there has been a sequential delivery of messages for humanity by the Creator God Delivery System—the Celestial UPS. The delivery has not just been through Jesus. There have been many deliveries, many teachers.

The Peacemaker, who traveled from the Huron people to help the warring Iroquois people find peace a very, very long time ago, is another one of those messengers. Precocious, reputedly born of virgin birth, he moved into his mission about the age of fourteen. Because he had a speech impediment, Hiawatha served as his interpreter. Through the Peacemaker's intervention the Seneca, Oneida, Onondaga, Cayuga, and Mohawk tribes were able to establish long-lasting peace through a well-balanced system of governance that included women as equals. The original Constitution of the United States, modeled upon the Iroquois Confederacy, lacked one key ingredient: women in equal partnership in the decision-making process. Our colonial ancestors obviously had a different attitude about women than the Iroquois.

In 2004, I was fortunate to hear Mohawk Chief Jake Swamp tell an abbreviated version of this epic story during an Iroquois teaching time at the Parliament of World Religions in Barcelona, Spain. It is an important story, one we can learn from, because the system works when properly constructed and used. An audio recording by Jake Swamp called *The Peacemaker's Journey: How the Great Law of Peace Came to the Original Five Nations* can be obtained online.

Jesus' teachings in their original form were peace teachings. He sought to prepare us for this time. As a student of Eastern teachings, having spent time in India, he would have learned about the end of the Kali Yuga along with esoteric teachings about the soul and spirit. It appears that the stage for now was set two thousand years ago, that Jesus taught us truths about ourselves and about what we have come to accomplish as souls. The first part of his mission had to take place on the physical stage. The second part, which is occurring in the spiritual realms, is happening now. The veils between the physical and spiritual worlds have been dissolving. This is why an increasing number of us are having paranormal encounters.

I have long believed that the Christ energy is within us, that the Second Coming has to do with our inner reconnection with the Christ (love) that we are, that the keys and the codes for this supra-ordinate state of being are contained within every fiber of our being. I do not confine this Christ energy to any religion. I do not believe that there are chosen and non-chosen people. I believe that the opportunity to reclaim oneself from soul enslavement is for everyone, that we are all children of God and, therefore, we are all chosen ones.

***

Turkey was a provocative travel experience for me. Mary's skillful guidance led me to an unexpected, deeper appreciation for the ministry and message of her son. The thought recently arose that it was time to learn more about Stella Maris, the name spoken to me during my first visit to the Casa de Dom Inacio in 2005. Mary has many names. The Latin title, Stella Maris, surfaced during the ninth century as a symbol of hope, guidance, and protection for seafarers.[19] What a perfect, deftly placed clue to pursue. I believe that she wanted me to understand that she, as Stella Maris, is guiding us to the second coming of the Christ, which is the activation of the Christ energy within each of us. We are the second coming of the Christ. Her light serves as an enormous beacon to we seafarers bobbing upon the waves of the great sea of change.

Thank you for meandering through worlds and time with me. With great pleasure, I now will explain the title of this book. Like other clues, the two-word title dropped into my consciousness as the book neared completion.

The story of Pandora's Box comes from Greek mythology. Another dramatic tale from the soap opera lives of the Greek gods and goddesses, this is an important story, for from this tale we learn the Greek version of the biblical story of Adam and Eve. The saga begins when a Titan named Prometheus, who had a tender place in his heart for mortal humans, stole the secret of fire and gave it to them. Enraged, the god Zeus ordered a terrible punishment for Prometheus. Tied to a rock and unprotected, his liver became daily food for a great eagle. This was an agonizing eternal sentence since his liver regenerated each day. Having duly dealt with Prometheus, Zeus next decreed that Hephaestus create a woman named Pandora to punish humankind. Made from clay, Pandora became the first woman to live among men. Pandora received many gifts of seduction from several gods and goddesses. Knowing that Zeus would inflict further punishment, Prometheus warned his brother Epimetheus not to accept any gifts from Zeus. Predictably, Epimetheus did not listen. He fell in love with and married Pandora (the gift). Zeus gave Pandora a box (actually, it was a jar) with explicit instructions that it not be opened. Being curious, as he knew she would be, she opened the lid. Evils, trials, and tribulations of all sorts that humankind had not previously experienced were set loose from the jar. Pandora, like Eve, became the "bad girl" who unleashed untold suffering into the world. However, it seems that there was hope at the bottom of the box if the lid was set back in place in a timely manner.[20]

A logical conclusion to be drawn is that once the jar-box of evil is completely empty, you must slam the lid back on before anything else can slide in. Voila, empty box, light without dark, holy vessel free of the manipulations of the demiurges. Amen! Which begs the question: if the lid must stay on the box to keep the interior pure, how do we know the light is within? This is where faith and trust come in. Setting aside the derogatory attitude toward and misuse of woman inherent in the story, the goal to be achieved, the hope, is not unlike what is asked of us currently—that we empty ourselves of that which is not light so that the light that is who we are can shine on without impediment.

The longstanding period of male domination that began in the most ancient of times received the fuel it needed with this story. Woman as seductress distracts man from his innocent relationship with God.

Blamed for all the suffering, woman is held responsible for the evil that runs rampant in the world. In this way, the seeds of disrespect for women took deeper root in the western world. Judaism and Christianity have their version of this story. Lilith, first wife of Adam, wanted equality in their relationship. This included sexual equality. Adam had other ideas. He believed in the missionary position—man on top, woman on the bottom. Lilith's response was to take off, make a new life. Subsequently held responsible for giving birth to the demons, one must ask with whom Lilith procreated, since the stories tell us that she and Adam were the only two people on the planet. According to Jewish folklore, she mated with the fallen archangel Samael. Samael walks both ways; he serves the light, he serves the dark. The Old Testament story tells us that Adam and Eve were the only ones in existence. Obviously, this was not the case. The first marriage contract ended, Eve arrived on the scene to become Adam's second wife. Eve, as we all know, ate of the apple. Again, the world was doomed and the blame heaped upon woman.

Yet the story has an even older wrinkle, one that goes all the way back to Sumeria, Mesopotamia and the *Epic of Gilgamesh*. A storm demon named Lilitu (Lilith) existed during Sumerian times. She was associated with the wind. Ancient belief was that she brought disease, illness and death. Thus, the story of woman gone amuck, wreaking havoc for humans is part of the earliest known records for this cycle of planetary inhabitation.[21]

In spite of the above, there have been periods of honoring the Mother, of cherishing the divine feminine. The ruins of the Cybele and Artemis temples remind us of such times. Temples to Isis and the Temple of Delphi do, as well. Two of the oldest known freestanding stone temples in the world still stand on the island of Gozo. Situated in the Mediterranean Sea, Gozo lies close to the better-known island of Malta. Called Gigantia, the temples are actually two full-figured representations in stone of the Mother Goddess. Visitors physically enter into the temples through her pelvis. A fine archeological discovery was that of a small stone full-bodied figurine called the "Sleeping Goddess." People travel to Gozo from all around the world to honor and to awaken the Sleeping Goddess. During our visit to Malta and Gozo in 2002, the tour guide told us that the women of these islands are particularly strong, substantial, and smart. Because they live in proximity to ancient structures that revere the feminine, and because women's sacred ceremonies have continued, her comment made absolute sense.

My personal story quickly fast-forwards after the 1985 Inner Child workshop when the lid came off my personal Pandora's Box. As the contents of the once-sealed box rose to the surface in methodical, preordained order, I retrieved the memory of the end of my life as priestess during the waning of Sumerian times. In fine whodunit fashion, I learned that my present life father was my killer. We incarnated together this lifetime for the healing of that stuck in time wounded feminine aspect of my soul.

Now I can answer the question posed back in 1991 while in talking circle during an intense 10-day retreat in the north woods of Canada. One of the facilitators asked, "Can you thank your father?" At the time, I did not know all the details, lifetimes of details, that hung between Dad and me. I was angry for other reasons. The answer was "No." Current lifetime issues had been the focus that led to that answer. I had to get to the original cause to be able to forgive, then express gratitude. Now I can say, without hesitation, "Thanks, Dad."

My little story is a mini version of what I believe is taking place at the mega level. All of humanity has been involved in the long saga of the killing and diminishment of the archetypal feminine principle. This squashing, as we can see, has had dire consequences for both sexes through the extreme imbalance it has created. We have lived far too long in a world of war. What is without is within. What is above is below.

Mary has demonstrated through the constancy of her love that the Mother, ever-present, is unstoppable. She—Mother—is resurrected. She speaks to those who will listen. She loves us so much she will not stop appearing, trying to get our attention. Serving as comforting mother, as healer, and encourager from the spirit realms, she reaches far beyond the bounds of religion to touch innumerable hearts and souls. Untold numbers of individuals, male and female, are aware of her guiding sweet presence, know her, feel her, call upon her without hesitation, and report profound encounters with her. She shows us who we really are. She calls to all of us to return to her son's teachings about love, soul, and spirit. Why ever would we resist the return to love? We know how different love and hatred feel.

During this leg of the journey, I have been fortunate to participate in ceremonies that honor the feminine, some led by male elders on ancient sacred sites, some led by women around home garden maypoles. A few were specifically to quicken the wake-up of the suppressed feminine principle.

Two years ago, I attended three days of instruction by the Dalai Lama at Indiana University. His Holiness started the teaching by stressing the importance to the human of mother love. He emphasized that it is mother love that nurtures the human heart and that humanity needs this love to survive. The beautifully crafted documentary DVD, *For the Next 7 Generations*, features the work and travels of the International Council of 13 Indigenous Grandmothers. Included in the DVD is a portion of their meeting with the Dalai Lama at his home in Dharamsala, India. In that clip, His Holiness counsels the grandmothers about the love only a mother can give, how special, how essential that love is. He speaks about the importance of the wisdom gained through life experience that the grandmothers have to impart. Obviously, the reinstatement of mother love is necessary for there to be any balance in the world.

The sleeping aspect of me, as priestess killed at the end of Sumerian times, is out of the box. Mother Mary has never really been in the box despite attempts to ensure that it was so. The Sleeping Goddess is out of the box. Sleeping Beauty is out of the box. I believe that the men who encouraged the women to lead the Rosary at the parish were out of the box, that at some level they recognized how important it is to encourage women to become equal partners in prayer. They wanted the women to get out of the box.

Mary is pronouncing through her appearances that we do not have to live life anymore in the paradigm that has been the Fourth World of duality. She asks us to move beyond divisiveness to bring forth a world of unity. She points clearly at geographic areas, nations, organizations, and peoples in grave distress. She has been calling for relentless love through prayer and fasting to address this eons old conundrum.

When we wholeheartedly, individually and collectively, do our inner work, the booby traps and stories of the past that were once stuffed into the box will cease to obstruct us. Without doubt, it is more than easy for us to fall back into well-rutted behavioral, thought, and emotional patterns. Regression takes less effort than what is required to embark with steadfast discipline upon a new path. Psyche and soul know those old maps very well. If it helps, think of the goal as being one of reconnecting yourself with your true path after a long period of paddling marshy, serpentine tributaries that provided momentary pleasure but inevitably dead-ended and tired you out. Integrate what you have learned from those side trips. The learning will not go to waste.

Now, paddle forward out of Plato's Cave with powerful strokes to greet the rising sun. There is no need for despair. Go forward into the brilliant light. Surrounded by those who love us unconditionally we are ushered, guided, and loved onto this path of return. Kali Yuga is a 26,000-year-old cycle that is ending. Thank goodness. The Fourth World of duality is ending. Hallelujah! Having taken on embodiment for this grand event, it behooves us to fearlessly wake up so that we can enjoy, wide-eyed and alert, the great drama as we participate in its conclusion. With the emptying of our personal Pandora's boxes, we make room for something new, something mysterious, something exciting and yet unknowable.

FULL CIRCLE

The year 2009 was a big one personally. In August, I participated in a weekend of ceremonial dance under the starry skies of Montana led by elders and medicine people I very much trust. During the dance, I was "taken out," meaning that I went into the spirit realms for an encounter. Instantly I went from dancing on my feet to falling splat on my face on the damp horse pasture—cleared, thank heavens—that was the dance arena. Although out of my body, I was in a fully conscious altered state. For the first time ever, I met Luther Standing Bear, Oglala Sioux Chief who crossed over into spirit in 1939. I had not known his name, did not know anything about him prior to that moment. Standing alongside him was Wallace Black Elk. Descended from Nicholas Black Elk, the great Lakota visionary, Wallace Black Elk was a much-loved Lakota elder, carrier of the Chanupa (sacred pipe), and international teacher who traveled to the other side in 2004. I had met Wallace Black Elk during a dance in Maine back in the 1990's.

Until that moment, my dance had been one of reliving the final days of freedom for the Lakota nation, watching the killing of the massive herds of life-giving buffalo, experiencing the Wounded Knee Massacre. Earlier the same weekend I had finally given away my well-worn yellowed copy of the famous book about the massacre. I had carried *Bury My Heart at Wounded Knee* since college. Standing above me, Luther Standing Bear and Wallace Black Elk looked at each other and said, "What are we going to do with her?" Then they said to me, "See? We're doing just fine. Let it go." They were referring to my anger about this terrible chapter of history. I knew they were right to urge me to let go the angry warrior pose. The anger was getting me nowhere but going round in circles. I told them, "Okay," and let the anger go. They faded away. I returned to full body consciousness.

Since shedding that angry burden, I have felt a refreshing lightness of being. When I committed to the dance, I knew only that it was important to attend. None of what transpired was due to conscious consideration or intent. My Divine Self took me to the dance. It knew what needed to happen, set the stage for this soul healing by pushing me to attend. Thus orchestrated, the weekend flowed seamlessly.

Next came a time of deep sharing at a Women's Council in October. I announced to this treasured community, without pre-thought, that I was finally laying down my sword. The time of fighting was over. It was time to move forward in Love. I gave up my sword for Love. With this pronouncement, the old, old, old Native American woman who joined me in song during Vision Quest in 1990 and later rode her horse into my bedroom said farewell and left. I saw her lift up, then fade away. I had known that she was in some way connected with Wounded Knee, but that was all. Grandmother had been guiding me for nineteen years to heal from the trauma of Wounded Knee and other indigenous tragedies. I was stunned. I truly had no idea that she had been working behind the scenes for so long. I did not know that she would accompany me to Council. The vision quest was finally complete.

Since 1992, my spiritual name has been Silent Woman. I received that name during a weekend long indigenous dance ceremony in New York City in 1992—the very same dance that called me to the horse pasture in Montana in 2009.   At the same time Silent Woman popped into my awareness, a lustrous opalescent gray bead landed at my feet. The lovely Taino grandmother who stood beside me acknowledged the bead gifting with a smile and a nod of her head. Genuinely awed, after a while I began to wonder about the name, what it implied. When I returned home, I asked if we could change it to Quiet Woman. That way I could talk. Instantly the whole house shook in a mighty "No!" response. Humbled, I contritely expressed gratitude. A few days later, I performed a private seaside ceremony to accept and activate the name. To my delight, other-dimensional dolphins attended. Eyes wide open, I laughed with joy as they visibly arced in play over the waves.

Over the next seventeen years, my Wonderful Team periodically placed me on conversational lockdown to enforce periods of silence I did not know I needed. For instance, during a twenty-one day trek through Nova Scotia, Newfoundland and Labrador, the only conversations permitted were those to book lodging, order food, and get gas. After growing tired of talking to myself, I surrendered to the silence. From then on, wonders I would have missed if distracted by talking presented bountifully. I have grown in the silence, come to cherish the richness of silence. When silent, especially out in nature among the trees, the mountains, in or beside water, I feel alive in a way that is indescribable. I can hear better, see better. In the silence, answers and wisdom present in just right timing. Spirit names are gifts and teachers. They are not destinations, but rather containers for purposeful growth experiences. With Grandmother's departure after the laying down of the sword, a new spiritual name, Lucerne, dropped into my consciousness from the spiritual realms.

Disarmed with Love, grateful for the new name, I now paddle forward into the next phase. Silent Woman moved me from warrior to something yet to be experienced. During meditation I was informed that Lucerne means Light Bearer. I have no idea what changes and lessons this name will bring. Since 1985, the primary focus of my life has been the healing of my soul. Locating and putting to rest the original sources of anger, distrust and lack of forgiveness has surely lightened the load. I will continue to follow the juicy clues as I jump back into the river for the next set of adventures. Some of the clues have arrived during lucid moments in the middle of the night. The subject matter is surprising and interesting.

Namaste is now the mantra that guides me as I enter into each new day of life. I intend to greet everyone with the peaceful energy of Namaste, which means, "The God in me acknowledges and honors the God in you." Souls know this word. Consistently I find the gentle vibration of this sacred word acknowledged, whether I have spoken it aloud or from the silence of my mind.

NAMASTE!

In the energy of love, in the spirit that is Namaste,
I wish you God-speed on your fantastic journey.

I can't begin this book with "Once upon a time..." because, having laid down the sword and been gifted a new spiritual name, I've been delivered into totally strange, unfamiliar territory. Having completed the tasks set forth in my first vision quest, a quest that lasted nineteen years, I settled in with some courageous, loving family members in a little rural town in New England. Yes, I definitely must call them courageous because they had no idea how much I had changed over the years. An apt visual would be this proposed headliner for the local paper: "Crew member from the USS Enterprise, a command ship of the Intergalactic Federation of Light, comes to live amidst the inhabitants of rural New England." Our worldviews and belief systems were and still are universes apart. What eases the tension of opposites is that, no matter what, we love each other.

During the first year of this new life, I lived like a hermit. I worked on *Out of the Box, A Soul's Surprising Journey*, walked in the woods with the dogs, communicated with my subtle realm friends. I was totally isolated and disconnected from everything and everyone with whom I had anything in common. I couldn't travel, didn't have the money. I had been thoroughly grounded, much to the relief of my immediate family. They had worried, needlessly I thought, about my safety and whereabouts as I traveled the world without concern while enthusiastically engrossed in the thrill of the adventure, knowing, most of the time, that I was tenderly cared for and protected by my Wonderful Team. The enforced stillness after being on the go constantly was almost unbearable. Jumping out of my skin, I didn't know what to do with myself. Certainly my spiritual teacher, White Waters, was chuckling in the ethers. Master of stillness, this is what he had encouraged over the many long years of our relationship. With nowhere to go but inside, I felt trapped. Occasionally I wondered if I'd been put out to pasture, that I'd become obsolete as a light worker. The way I had known to work and live dried up like the desert.

There was no recourse but to surrender to this new experience. Turning back was not an option. Wings clipped, brought to my knees once again, I chafed and bucked to no avail. Change, even when quested for and then gifted by the spiritual realms in response, is disconcerting. The only logical choice left was to accept the unknown as I embarked upon a new, yet undefined quest. Moving into a little elfin-type tree house cottage situated above a tinkling stream helped. Surrounded by my friends, the trees, accompanied by the joyful chatter of the squirrels and chipmunks, I began to feel at home. I began to realize that the feeling of strangeness underscored the reality that something truly did shift with the new spiritual name and change of orientation from sword carrying light worker to light bearer. I have begun an entirely new relationship with myself.

Footnotes

1 http://en.wikipedia.org/wiki/Barnabas

2 www.newadvent.org/cathen/02300a.htm

3 *Medicine Cards*, Jamie Sams and David Carson, 1988, p. 213

4 http://en.wikipedia.org/wiki/Amazing_Grace

5 www.brasiliabrazil.info/sanctuary=dom-bosco-brasilia.html

6 http://en.wikipedia.org/wiki/John_Bosco#cite_ref-28--30

7 *A Light Shining on the Earth*, Edition du Signe, 1997

8 http://marieroseferron.catholicweb.com

9 *Bury My Heart at Wounded Knee*, Dee Brown, 1970

10 *The Holy Bible*, Exodus 20:13

11 http://peacepilgrim.fotopages.com

12 www.templartreasure.

13 *The Second Coming of Christ, The Resurrection of the Christ Within You*, Paramhansa Yogananda, 2004, pp.1514-151

14 http://en.wikipedia.org/wiki/Milarepa

15 http://en.wikipedia.org.wiki.Manichean

16 http://www.gnosis.org/naghamm/nhl_sbj.htm

17 http://Cathar.info/Cathars.htm

18 http://en.wikipedia.org/wiki/Inter_caetera

19 http://en.wikipedia.org/wiki/Our_Lady_Star_of_the_Sea

20 http://en.wikipedia.org/wiki/Pandora's_box

21 http://en.wikipedia.org/wiki/Lilit

Bibliography

A Light Shining on the Earth. Edition du Signe, 1997

Amorth, Father Gabriel: *An Exorcist Tells His Story.* Ignatius Press, 1999

Anderson, George: *We Don't Die.* Putnam Adult, 1988

Augustine of Hippo: *The Confessions of Saint Augustine.* Classic Books America, 2009

Austin, Lou: *The Little Me and the Great Me.* The Partnership Foundation WV, 1957

Barry, Brunonia: *The Map of True Places.* HarperCollins Publishers, 2010

Brown, Dee: *Bury My Heart at Wounded Knee.* Holt, Rinehart & Winston, 1970

Chopra, Deepak: *Magical Mind, Magical Body.* Audio Cassette, 1994

Chopra, Deepak: *The Return of Merlin.* Ballantine Books, 1996

Fell, Barry: *America B.C.* Pocket Books, 1978

For the Next 7 Generations, DVD. Hartley Film Foundation, 2008

Frankl, Viktor: *From Death-Camp to Existentialism.* Beacon Press, 1961

Homer, Bernard Knox and Robert Fagles: *The Iliad.* Penguin Classics Deluxe Edition, 1998

Illibagiza, Immaculee: *Left to Tell.* Hay House, 2007

Mack, Dr. John: *Abduction, Human Encounters with Aliens.* Scribner, 1994

Madgalena, Flo Aeveia: *I Remember Union: The Story of Mary Magdalena.* All Worlds Publishing, 1992

Morehouse, Dr. David: *Psychic Warrior: Inside the CIA's Stargate Program, The True Story of a Soldier's Espionage and Awakening.* St. Martin's Paperbacks, 1998

Mortenson, Greg: *Three Cups of Tea.* Penguin Books, 2007

Ostrander, Sheila and Lynn Schroeder: *Psychic Discoveries.* Marlowe & Company, 1997

Plato: *The Republic,* translated by Francis MacDonald Cornford. Oxford University Press, 1945

Robert, Henry M.: *Robert's Rules of Order: Revised.* Morrow Quill Paperbacks, 1979

Rowling, J.K.: *Harry Potter and the Sorcerer's Stone.* Scholastic, 1998

Sams, Jamie and David Carson: *Medicine Cards: The Discovery of Power Through the Ways of Animals.* Bear & Co, 1988

Sams, Jamie and Twylah Nitsch: *Other Council Fires Were Here Before Ours.* Harper Collins, 1992

Sora, Steven: *The Last Colony of the Templars.* Destiny Books, 2004

Swann, Ingo: *Great Apparitions of Mary: An Examination of Twenty-Two Supranormal Appearances.* Crossroad Classic, 1996

Swamp, Jake: *The Peacemaker's Journey: How the Great Law of Peace Came to the Original Five Nations.* Parabola Audio, 1996

Tazewell, Charles: *The Littlest Angel.* Children's Press, Inc, 1946

Tolkien, J.R.R.: *The Lord of the Rings.* Ballantine Books, 1970

Twyman, James: *The Secret of the Beloved Disciple.* Findhorn Press, 2000

Warner, Marian: *Alone of All Her Sex.* Littlehampton Book Services Ltd, 1976

Watzlawick, Dr. Paul: *Change: Principles of Problem Formation and Problem Resolution.* W.W. Norton & Company, 1974

Whitfield, Dr. Charles: *Healing the Child Within: Discovery and Recovery for Adult Children of Dysfunctional Families,* Health Communications, Inc., 1987

Williams, Terry Tempest: *Finding Beauty in a Broken World.* Pantheon, 2008

Xavier, Francisco Candido: *Nosso Lar.* Conselho Espirita Internacional, 2006

Xavier, Francisco Candido: *Paul and Stephen, by the Spirit Emmanuel.* Conselho Espirita Internacional, 2008

Yogananda, Paramhansa: *The Second Coming of Christ, The Resurrection of the Christ Within You.* Self-Realization Fellowship, 2004

Resources

Sandy Akers
Energy Healing; workshops for awakening and becoming your own true self.
505-699-8995
www.sandyakers.com

Barbara Brennan School Of Healing
College specializing in hands-on healing and personal transformation.
www.barbarabrennan.com

Bennie Le Beau
Earth Wisdom Foundation
http://tetonrainbows.com

Cahokia Mounds
30 Ramey Street, Collinsville, IL 62234
618-346-5160
http://cahokiamounds.org

Cherokee National Museum
Willis Road, Tahlequah, OK 74464
918-456-6007
http://www.cherokeeheritage.org

Christ In The Desert Benedictine Monastery
In northern New Mexico, a remote location for meditative retreat.
P.O. Box 270, Abiquiu, NM 87510
801-545-8567
http://christdesert.org

EMDR Institute, Inc
A comprehensive integrative psychological method for healing trauma.
PO Box 750, Watsonville, CA 95077
831-761-1040
www.emdr.vom

Flo Aeveia Magdalena
Soul Support Systems
802-463-2200
www.soulsupportsystems.org
soulsupportsystems@comcast.org

His Holiness Gayuna Sundima Cealo
Foundation for Global Harmony USA
Direct action projects to empower people
Spiritual development
http://www.cealo.net

John of God
Spiritual healing
Abadiania, Brazil
www.FriendsoftheCasa.info

La-Ho-Chi Institute
Energy healing and spiritual transformation
Directors: Dan Watson, Ph.D. and Beloved
828-698-1448
www.laho-chi.com

Little Rose Apostolate
http://marieroseferron.catholicweb.com
beatification@verizon.net

Medjugorje, Bosnia
www.medjugorje.org

Dr. Norma Milanovich
Athena Leadership Center
http:ourtrustisingod.com
info@athena/ctr.com

Museum of the Cherokee Indian
589 Tsali Boulevard, Cherokee, NC 28719
828-497-3481
http://www.cherokeemuseum.org

National Shrine of the Divine Mercy
2 Prospect Hill Road, Eden Hill, Stockbridge, MA 01262
413-298-3931
www.thedivinemercy.org/shrine

National Shrine of Our Lady of the Snows
442 S. De Mazenod Drive, Belleville, IL 62223
800-682-2879
http://snows.org

National Shrine of St. Elizabeth Ann Seton
333 South Seton Avenue, Emmetsburg, MD 21727
301-447-6606
www.setonshrine.org

North Carolina Outward Bound
Wilderness challenge and adventure courses.
www.ncobs.org

Omega Institute
Retreats and workshops
Rhinebeck, NY
480-767-5346
http://eomega.org

RwandanH.U.G.S.
Non-profit ministry started by Nancy Strachan; supports empowering,
revitalizing projects for people in Rwanda.
540-586-4446
Rwandanhugs@aol.com

Sathya Sai Baba
Avatar whose ashram is located in Puttaparthi, India at Prasanthi
Nilayam; the 2nd incarnation of a 3-part incarnation series that began with
Shirdi Sai Baba and will complete with Prema Baba.
http://www.srisathyasai.org.in
radiosai.org

Selene
Energy healing and teachings
303-494-8802
Selene.HealingArts@gmail.com

Wolf Clan Teaching Lodge
Grandmother Twylah Nitsch's legacy, carried forward by her son, Bob Nitsch, and daughter-in-law Lee.
http://wolfclanteachinglodge.org

Gabrielle Spencer, D.D.
Alternative Healing Practitioner, Advanced Theta Healing Practitioner, Bioresonance & Feedback (CBBT) Therapist Energetix CoReSystem
480-567-8491
www.ra-energetix.com

Tierra Wools
Teaching and retail cooperative dedicated to supporting the local community while preserving the art of rug-weaving.
91 Main Street, Los Ojos, NM 87551
575-588-7231
www.handweavers.com

Upledger Institute
Home base for CraniSacral Therapy
Palm Beach Gardens, FL
800-233-5880
www.upledger.com

Glossary

Absolute: the perfect, complete, pure heart of creation. The alpha and omega, the source beyond all known source.

Archangel: a chief angel in the celestial hierarchy.

Ascended Masters: spiritually enlightened masters who once were ordinary humans and who remain in service to humanity.

Avatar: the incarnation of God in human form.

Bodhisattva: term for enlightened beings who, having completed the lessons presented to them by Earth School, compassionately assist others to do the same.

Christ Consciousness: the state of consciousness where one realizes union in divine love; this is the consciousness of love that is at the center of Jesus' teachings.

Curandero: Meso-American term for spirit-guided healers who have dedicated their lives to the treatment of physical and spiritual illnesses. The range of practices can be diverse and may include the use of eggs for divination, herbs for smudging and healing, journeying in spirit, channeling healing spirits, ritual cleansing with alcohol and fire.

Divine Self: term the author has come to use to describe the true self, the pure essence of creation that not only inhabits the body, but also extends beyond the limitations of the body. It is that which oversees and orchestrates our earthly development and spiritual curriculum. The concepts of higher or lower self are inadequate to define this essence. I defer to Grandmother Twylah's teachings to go within rather than look outside of ourselves to find our true essence. What we seek is within, guides from within.

Epicurean School of Philosophy: the teachings of Epicurus, who eschewed the idea of divine intervention and proposed that tranquility and freedom from fear could be achieved through knowledge, friendship, virtuous living and moderation.

Evil: that which has turned away from God; non-loving energies

God: the pulse of life that is contained within every living thing throughout this and all the universes. God is androgynous, is Mother-Father, is unified Oneness.

Harry Potter School: refers to schooling that teaches a metaphysical curriculum such as Hogwarts does in Rowling's Harry Potter books. Such schools certainly do exist!

Hierarchy of Light: the group of angels, archangels, masters of light that assists humans from the spiritual realms.

Higher Self: another term for the self that exists beyond worldly existence. Also called the divine self or the true self.

Inipi: Lakota term for the purification ceremony more commonly known by the term "sweat lodge." Inipi is one of the seven sacred rites given to the Lakota people by White Buffalo Calf Woman. Participants enter into a lodge made of saplings and covered, usually by blankets, to create total darkness inside to represent the womb of Mother Earth. Red-hot stones, prayerfully placed one at a time into a pit inside the lodge, receive a water blessing that creates a cleansing steam. The entire ceremony is a prayer.

Jungian Anaylsis: the form of psychotherapy, developed by Dr. Carl Jung, that explores the imagination through dream analysis and the experiences of daily life.

Shamanism: the oldest healing tradition in the world. Trained to communicate with the physical and spiritual worlds for healing purposes, shamans utilize specific rituals to assist with the healing goal. Training is intense and arduous.

Soul Retrieval: the process of discovering, then reintegrating parts of one's soul that have become stuck, lost or disconnected through the unfinished business of past lives as well as current life and traumatic events.

Stopped Time Incidents: describes when an individual or group has stepped out of ordinary time to have an experience or encounter that is otherworldly. Time can stand still, go backwards or forwards. Usually there are obvious indicators that mark such an event—ie., a perfectly working clock inexplicably jumps forward an hour or curiously stops only to later restart. The "stopped time" is to help the experiencer take notice that something extraordinary has occurred.

Sri Yantra: an intricate, visually geometric representation of the Divine Mother.

Vision Quest: indigenous practice that involves prayers and fasting while alone in a wilderness location for the purpose of making a deep connection with the spirit world. The goal is to receive a vision that will guide one's life purpose.

Wonderful Team: author's name for the group of guides, angels, masters of light, archangels who provide personalized assistance and training from the spiritual realms.

ABOUT THE AUTHOR

Barbara has settled into a tiny tree-house cottage that sits above a tinkling stream in the great state of New Hampshire. Living among the trees, the many lakes and mountains that are abundant with wildlife, she continues to integrate the lessons from her spiritual odyssey while opening to the mystery that is her new life. While long retired from a career in psychotherapy, she does enjoy being part of a local hospice team.

Made in the USA
Monee, IL
03 February 2024

52325401R00118